Marriage
Is Like
Dancing

RICHARD C. EYER

CONCORDIA PUBLISHING HOUSE · SAINT LOUIS

To my wife, who sometimes leads, but mostly follows

Published 2007 by Concordia Publishing House
3558 S. Jefferson Ave., St. Louis, MO 63118-3968
1-800-325-3040 • www.cph.org

Text © 2007 Richard C. Eyer

Manufactured in the United States of America

Library of Congress Cataloging-in-Publication Data
Eyer, Richard C., 1939-
  Marriage is like dancing / Richard C. Eyer.
     p. cm.
  Includes bibliographical references.
  ISBN-13: 978-0-7586-1302-8
  ISBN-10: 0-7586-1302-4
  1. Marriage--Religious aspects--Christianity. 2. Ballroom
dancing--Miscellanea. I. Title.

  BV835.E95 2007
  248.8'44--dc22

2006027766

1 2 3 4 5 6 7 8 9 10   16 15 14 13 12 11 10 09 08 07

Contents

Preface

They say one should write about the things one knows best. Next to my relationship with Jesus Christ, my marriage is the thing I know best. This is not to say I have a perfect understanding of all the dynamics operative in my marriage, but I do value my marriage above all other endeavors in my life. This book is not intended to help couples with a seriously flawed marriage. Marital counseling would be a better choice, perhaps with this book as a follow-up as things improve. One of my colleagues reviewed this manuscript before publication and expressed the opinion that this would be a good book for people with a basically good marriage that can always use tweaking. I would add that it might also be a good book for those newlyweds who want to get started in building a good marriage.

The only research acquired for this book is the knowledge obtained through forty years of marriage, ten years as a pastor performing premarital and marital counseling, and twenty years as a hospital chaplain at the bedside listening to people talk about their lives. Although my understanding of marriage is grounded in objective biblical studies, when I thought of writing about the application of these studies to my own marriage I was apprehensive, fearing that I might give the impression that my marriage was the ideal to follow. I have tried to reduce this presumption by including references to my own difficulties and failings in offering the kind of leadership required of a husband. I also attempt to insert humor along the way to lighten my own seriousness about the subject, as well as the reader's.

George Vaillant of Harvard Medical School has coined the term "Keeper of the meaning" to describe a developmental stage

The partnership in dancing seems so obvious a parallel to the partnership between husband and wife.

in life in which a person has a need to pass on to others that which has been meaningful and worthwhile in his own life. Perhaps I am at that stage, passing on what marriage means to me, as Adam did in making the observation concerning his wife-to-be, Eve, in saying, "This at last is bone of my bones and flesh of my flesh . . . " (Genesis 2:23).

Although I write from a man's perspective, I realize that few men are likely to pick up and read a book on marriage, much less one that uses the metaphor of ballroom dancing. Therefore, it is my hope that wives will read and discuss this book with their husbands. She may even suggest to him that he read it for her sake and for the benefit of their marriage. To this end, I have included chapter discussion guides at the end of the book for husbands and wives to use together. I would NOT suggest that these discussion guides be used for group discussion because the questions need to be answered in private by each couple. It is better that these things be discussed in private where feelings and trust can be built between husband and wife. In some cases a husband will not be willing to talk about his marriage. Nevertheless, I believe that a wife will benefit from this book in gaining a better understanding of how to support her husband appropriately taking the lead in their marriage. Finally, it is my hope that this book will be helpful to married couples and to the ongoing discussion of marriage as something created by God and not by a society. Those who wish to support this belief do best to live their own marriages in witness to it.

The use of the metaphor of ballroom dancing to describe marriage is the product of two intensive years of dance lessons and hard practice that my wife and I have undertaken at a local Fred Astaire Dance Studio. Almost immediately upon beginning lessons, I saw ballroom dancing as a description of marriage. The partnership in dancing seems so obvious a parallel to the partnership between husband and wife. Those who have taken ballroom dance lessons and enjoy dancing will appreciate the learning process I narrate. Those who don't dance may find the metaphor cumbersome, but I hope readers might be encouraged to consider dance lessons simply because they are enjoyable and certainly a good exercise.

God has given marriage as a sign of something eternal . . .

Each chapter opens with a story about dancing, which will lead in to a discussion on the aspects of marriage. Paralleling these stories, I will examine passages from both Old and New Testaments to show that God has given marriage as a sign of something eternal, namely the icon of the relationship between God and all those He made and called into a faith relationship with Himself.

I am eager to thank those who have been our instructors in dance. Russell Larson and Angie Kluth, who are top professional competitors in dance, have shown us the delight and wonder of ballroom dance. Their patience and creativity in teaching old dogs new tricks will be appreciated. There were also many fellow students at the Studio who became new friends in support of our efforts to learn to dance. Colleagues, neighbors, and friends who at my request read and gave feedback on the developing manuscript, also deserve thanks. I owe special thanks to Nathan Jastram, scholar and friend, whose studies on the image of God have helped me understand what it means to be made male and female, and whose editing of my writing helped both correct and clarify much. My daughter, Mary Loy, who has inherited my forthrightness, has also been helpful in correcting my syntax and encouraging me to get to the point in my writing. Working with my publishing editor, Scot Kinnaman, has also been a pleasure. We not only seem to be on the same wavelength in our discussions of processing the manuscript, but he has revealed that he is a kindred spirit in that he and his wife have also taken a few dance lessons. Finally, I say thank you to my wife, who, having put up with my idiosyncrasies in trying to learn how to lead, has always been my inspiration for wanting to learn how to dance. Dancing a waltz with my wife in the confines of our living room while listening to music we both love remains a delight!

Introduction

There are many good books on marriage. This book is special because it examines marriage in the context of what it means to be created in the image of God and tries to apply that to marriage with the metaphor of ballroom dancing. The image of God is first and foremost about holiness lost in Adam and regained in Christ, but it is also about what it means to be a man and woman in this world as God intended us to be. It is therefore the foundation of how we are to live, especially in marriage.

Chapter 1 defines marriage on the basis of the biblical theme of men and women made in the image of God as well as the theme of the one flesh union between husband and wife. This first chapter is foundational to what follows, and is important as our society wrestles with the possibility of redefining marriage to accommodate to a changing culture. Marriage is not however a culture chooses to define it. Marriage is an institution created by God for a man and a woman.

The second chapter addresses the issue of leadership in marriage and takes the direction of the biblical model of the husband as the one who leads and the wife as one who follows, as happens in ballroom dancing. The not-so-easy challenge of this biblical model is discussed in deciphering what it actually means to lead and what it means to follow. I have tried to be sensitive to the varying ways couples have worked this out for themselves, but I argue for the essential vocation of the husband as the

> Marriage is not merely however a culture chooses to define it. Marriage is an institution created by God for a man and a woman.

. . . a husband and wife are together and individually part of the body of Christ.

one who must take responsibility for the marriage and home he has been called by God to lead.

Chapter 3 deals with conflict in marriage. Among other things, there is a discussion on how to argue well versus arguing badly. Arguing well is an art to be learned. It brings resolution to problems faced together by a husband and wife. Arguing badly is evidence of a human nature that needs redemption in Jesus Christ. Therefore, the substance of this chapter is about the necessity for a husband and wife to learn to practice confession and forgiveness between them in marriage.

Chapter 4 confronts the issue of sensuality between husband and wife. I have tried to distinguish between wholesome sensuality and unwholesome sensuality. The word sensuality is used to encompass sexuality and sexual intercourse, but it also includes the courtesy, sensitivity, tenderness, and affection toward each other that is displayed in public as well as in the bedroom. The premise is that sensuality, which serves the expression and growth of the one flesh union, is a wholesome sensuality.

In chapter 5 the spiritual connections between husband and wife are explored. Both public worship and personal devotions are essential as a backdrop for all that marriage is about because a husband and wife are together and individually part of the body of Christ. The delicate issue of the relationship between a Christian married to a non-Christian is also addressed by means of the writings of St. Paul.

Chapter 6 is a discussion about the necessity of making time for each other at home alone. I will spell out how a good marriage is a blessing to the world, offering service and hope to others. Included here is a candid discussion of the problem of infidelity in marriage.

Chapter 7 discusses aging well together as husband and wife, and preparing for the reality that one spouse will likely die before the other. Preparing for death does not mean escaping the pain caused by the loss of the other, but to be able to talk about it as part of the intimacy of marriage. Although I cannot speak from personal experience about losing a spouse, I can speak from the point of anticipating the death of a spouse. My wife and I do anticipate and speak about this, sharing our conviction that we must each learn to love God more than we love each other in order to continue living well when the other is gone.

Finally, chapter 8 explores the topic of parenting in three different ways. I speak to the need for young couples to re-parent themselves, to parent their children well, and maybe to parent their parents someday. Being prepared for all three kinds of parenting is important in a marriage.

Afterword

Although it will be obvious that topics in this book have been shared between my wife, Susan, and me in endless conversations over eighteen months of writing, I asked her to read it and write a response to the final manuscript to be included as the Afterword. My wife's having the last word is the equivalent of the woman taking her bow at the end of a performance waltz, as is the custom. I happily step aside to enable her to do so.

marriage is

MARRIAGE IS LIKE DANCING

My parents met on the dance floor in 1934. They continued to dance through nearly six decades of marriage until Dad died at age 94. For them, dancing primarily meant the waltz, fox-trot, rumba, cha-cha, and other Latin dances. Last summer, after nearly forty years of marriage, and for the first time in each of our lives, my wife and I began taking ballroom dancing lessons at a Fred Astaire Dance Studio. I had often told my wife about an elderly clergyman in my youth who tried to convince a group of us young men that dancing is a sin. He declared that if we had to dance, it should be only after marriage and, even then, only in the privacy of the bedroom with one's own wife.

ike dancing

That point of view brought to mind several thoughts and images at the time. My first thought was that my parents had danced most Saturday nights when I was growing up and had never missed attending church the next morning. I could see nothing wrong with their love of dancing or any lack of faithfulness to each other or to God in worship. Following quickly, I had an image of being married someday. I imagined my wife and I in our bedroom, and it struck me that the least of my desires at that time would be to ask my wife for the next dance. Finally, I came to the conclusion that if we did dance in our bedroom, according to my mentor, apparently the "sin" of dancing would then be acceptable. I concluded there was something wrong with the well-intentioned perspective of my honorable sage.

I can honestly say that my wife and I have never danced in our bedroom. Nevertheless, we did decide to take ballroom dance lessons for use on the dance floor. At the time, we were not interested in all types of dancing. Disco dancing, for example, not only brought to mind visions of an attempt by people our age to be young again, but I was also inclined to accept the judgment made by contemporary ballroom dancers that disco was already part of the Dark Ages. In disco, it seemed to this untrained eye, that having a partner mattered little, since each dancer did his own thing on the dance floor. My wife and I were also not interested in a style of dancing that is suggestive of something more appropriately done in the privacy of our bedroom without dancing. It was no doubt the sexual suggestiveness of some dances that prompted the advice given me by the elderly clergyman in my youth.

What prompted our interest in dancing as retirees was our two-week tour of Turkey and Greece during which we enjoyed a three-day cruise among the Greek islands. As is often the case, the evenings aboard ship provided opportunity for dancing. Although my wife and I had contrived to dance occasionally through the years, our attempt consisted mostly in learning to begin and end with the music. When we returned from the trip abroad, I said to my wife, "Honey, I'd like to learn how to dance!" She responded with a virtual wink and an adept presentation of a coupon for one free dance lesson she had stashed away for just an opportunity such as this.

. . . in ballroom dancing the man leads and the woman follows

So began our dance lessons, and we are still enjoying every minute of them. Learning to dance has been a challenge. It requires a studied focus on patterns and connections to each other. The daily practice has been a physical workout, both exhausting and satisfying. All in all, dancing has been a delight, even with its good and bad days—just like the challenge, the studied focus, and the daily exercise of our marriage.

We were told in our first lesson that in ballroom dancing the man leads and the woman follows. Our instructor was quick to point out that this does not mean the man coerces or shoves the woman around the dance floor, but rather that he "invites" her to follow him in their dance together. At first, this sounded to me like merely a politically correct way to describe what most men did on the dance floor, directing her to go where she might otherwise not have been inclined to go—in

. . . if she says yes to either dance or marriage, she must learn to follow just as he must learn to lead

effect, steering her around the floor like a tugboat in the harbor. However, the instructor was trying to show the courtesy of ballroom dancing. In today's ballroom dancing the woman may choose to follow the man or not, but, of course, the dance cannot continue unless she does. Therefore, if she wants to dance with him, it is her decision to follow him, just as it is her decision to say "yes" if she chooses to accept his invitation to marriage. And if she says yes to either dance or marriage, she must learn to follow just as he must learn to lead. Neither leading nor following comes naturally, and therein lies the benefits of dance lessons and the enrichment of marital counseling.

Although our instructor may not have realized that we were beginning to see dance as a metaphor for our marriage, he did point out that the woman may not change places with the man and lead him on the dance floor. Later on this was amended to explain that sometimes, when the woman steps forward and the man steps backward, the woman must lead, but only for a few planned steps until it is time for the man to resume his lead. It seemed to me, and my wife agreed, that marriage is a lot like dancing. The man ought to lead. But there are times when the wife must assume responsibility for a few steps before returning the lead to her husband. That is not an easy thing to do. It is human nature for both to want to lead rather than to follow. That is what so often causes marital disharmony. Neither leading nor following comes easily either in dancing or in marriage, and both husband and wife need to work at it together with daily practice.

This idea of the man leading and the woman following in marriage runs counter to everything that has been happening in the revision of gender roles in our culture. The energies of those who fear abuse by men have poured out as a militant resistance to the idea that a man should take any lead in marriage. Likewise, philosophical egalitarians have politicized marriage, claiming that the man and the woman must each assert leadership over their own lives and not presume to lead each other's. Implied in this assertion is the belief that the roles of men and women in marriage are simply a matter of culture and function, and not inherent by nature as given by God. It is not surprising that the functional-culturists believe the roles of men and women in marriage are easily interchangeable.

Fortunately, however prevalent this point of view may seem to be, few happily married couples really believe this. Under social pressure, married couples may try to make the current cultural model work, but seldom is this model fulfilling in the long run, and time and disappointment changes things again. Couples can attempt to do their own thing on the dance floor and in marriage, but ultimately the man still has to lead and the woman still has to follow in order for dancing or marriage to produce a stellar performance fulfilling to both as a couple. Understanding who leads and who follows is what makes marriage work for the benefit of men, women, and the children that come

Neither leading or following comes easily either in dancing or marriage . . .

Jesus said, "Love one another;" He did not say, "Dominate one another." from it. Where couples do exchange the lead, the woman often picks it up either because her husband will not responsibly do so, or because circumstances such as illness or handicap necessitate it, or because the woman as a strong personality cannot separate her leadership in the community from her following a lead in the marriage.

Now, before it sounds like I am proposing that men should "dominate" women in marriage and that women should subject themselves to the abusive dominance of men, let us reject both these thoughts. Jesus said, "Love one another"; He did not say, "Dominate one another." This applies throughout the whole experience of life, but most importantly in marriage. Jesus Christ is the true Word of God that became flesh and blood among us and transforms us to love, lead, and follow in marriage. In addition to being "the only begotten Son of God," He is also the heavenly Groom and we, the Church, His earthly Bride. (See Ephesians 5:25–33.)

THE GOSPEL AND MARRIAGE

The model for leading and following in marriage is the new relationship between Christ and His people, renewed daily through mutual confession and absolution. Jesus Christ, God the Son, demonstrated submission to God the Father in becoming obedient to death on the cross to reunite us to God. The authority of the Father and the submission of the Son redeemed our misuse of authority and submission, transforming each into a good to be experienced in marriage by God's grace. Christ's submission to death on the cross is God's work of reconciling the world to Himself, and the divorce between God and the world is repaired through faith in Jesus Christ.

Those who know the joy and promise of this authority and submission under God know it as a good thing to be embraced daily with eagerness. The wife is to submit to her husband "as to the Lord." The reminder, "as to the Lord," is as important for the husband as it is for the wife. "As to the Lord," reminds him that he stands under the authority of God as his wife submits to him. These words, "as to the Lord," make all the difference between a sinful authoritarianism and a fulfilling faithfulness to God for both husband and wife.

DEFINING MARRIAGE

If we are to understand what it means to lead and to follow in a way that brings fulfillment to a marriage, we must understand the institution of marriage itself. How shall we define marriage? That is currently the question under discussion in our society. Shall we recognize marriage as the union of one man and one woman? Shall we recognize marriage as the union of a man to another man or a woman to another woman, the gay marriage? Shall marriage be a promise of lifelong commitment before God and the community with which we are all one, or shall marriage be any two people, young or old, who choose to live together without a wedding or commitment for life, for sexual convenience or mutual financial benefit? Shall marriage be a contract for a set number of years, to be reviewed for its continuance or dissolved for other interests? Shall marriage be the prerequisite for procreation, or shall society support any unmarried

> . . . marriage is
> not whatever we
> choose to make it,
> but it is what God
> has made it to be

woman choosing to have a child with the assistance of a fertility clinic that provides donor sperm to fulfill her wishes? Is marriage little more than an invention of a culture and therefore something that needs to be revised from generation to generation, or is there something inherent in marriage itself that causes it to work best, among other reasons, when the husband leads and the woman follows?

The assertion of this book is that marriage is not whatever we choose to make of it, but it is what God has made it to be! Nearly all cultures, regardless of external customs, reflect something of the truth that marriage is from God at the core of their experience of marriage. There may be cultures where the leadership of the husband is little more than outright abuse of the wife and children, as well as cultures where a wife's assertion of authority is demeaning of the man, but these things merely highlight human nature at its worst. In our own culture, there are models of marriage that range from varieties of abuse to "anything goes" consensual agreements, but such variety does not give legitimacy to a belief in cultural relativism with regard to marriage. The institution of marriage has suffered the same attacks on its historic credibility as morality has from those who attempt to dismantle anything that hints of biblical origin. In this book, we will move beyond the debate with culturalists and return to an understanding of marriage as revealed and ultimately fulfilled in relationship to God, through Jesus Christ our Lord.

BIBLICAL THEMES OF MARRIAGE

The theme of marriage appears in the Bible again and again as a metaphor for the kind of relationship God creates between Himself and His faithful people. In the Old Testament, God reveals Himself as a faithful husband in pursuit of His repeatedly faithless wife, Israel. The testimony of the prophets throughout the Old Testament bears witness to Israel's constant unfaithfulness to God and adulterous exploration of pagan practices. God does not abandon Israel for her faithlessness, but pursues her into the New Testament by becoming a flesh and blood man who loves flesh and blood people of this world. It is because of unfaithfulness that God comes as a man, not to condemn, but in mercy as a loving parent comes to a child engaged in self-destructive behavior.

In the New Testament, God makes Himself known in His Son, Jesus Christ, the heavenly Bridegroom, who comes down to earth in pursuit of those He chooses to make one with Himself. We, who by our faith in Him are married to Christ, find our lives being transformed by Him. We learn from Christ what it means to follow as He leads us lovingly in our marriage to God. This model of learning to follow Christ's lead brings fulfillment to all of life. This marriage with God-in-Christ is a unique experience in life, and marriage between husband and wife is the mirror image of it on earth. No other relationship on

> No other relationship on earth, either between closest friends or between parent and child, is the same as the uniqueness of the relationship between husband and wife.

earth, either between closest friends or between parent and child, is the same as the uniqueness of the relationship between husband and wife. Basic themes in the Bible help us uncover some of the mystery and deeper meaning of marriage as God has given it to us to live.

MARRIAGE AND THE IMAGE OF GOD

The origin of the biblical understanding of marriage is found in the fact that man and woman were created in the image of God.[1] To be created in the image of God simply means that human beings were created to be like God, at least in some ways. This description of human identity is given in the first chapter of Genesis, the first book of the Bible. It is significant that this image of God theme sets the stage for all that follows in the Bible about the nature of the relationship between God and His created human beings. God says,

> Let us make man in our image, after our likeness. And let them have dominion over the fish of the sea and over the birds of the heavens and over the livestock and over all the earth and over every creeping thing that creeps on the earth. So God created man in his own image, in the image of God he created him; male and female he created them. (Genesis 1:26–27)

Human beings were created in the image of God. This means that we were to share in being like God. This does not

---

1.   This perspective draws on studies by Nathan Jastram, "Man as Male and Female: Created in the Image of God," *Concordia Theological Quarterly* (January 2004).

mean human beings were to be like God in all ways. God is God and we are His creation. Although there are many implications for what it means to have been made in the image of God, for our purposes we will explore only the way humans were created to be "like" God, that is, in the relationship between male and female as husband and wife.

God desires a married couple to reflect, like a mirror, the mutual love between Christ and His bride, the Church

In the Genesis account the one true God describes Himself in the plural, "Let us make man in our image," and then He is described in the singular as creating Man in "his own image." God is both singular and plural in that he is "one God in three persons."[2] The three persons of the Trinity—the Father, Son, and Holy Spirit—relate to one another in a bond of perfect love and harmony. God made man in His image as male and female, and in marriage the two become one flesh. God designed male and female to relate to each other in a bond of perfect love and harmony in marriage. God desires a married couple to reflect, like a mirror, the mutual love between Christ and His bride, the Church. Through faith in Christ, God enables us to know and to begin to live according to His intent for how male and female are to interact in marriage.

---

2. This phrase is from the Athanasian Creed, one of the three ecumenical creeds, along with the Apostle's Creed and the Nicene Creed, accepted by all Christians in content, if not always in form in non-creedal churches. God is one God who reveals Himself to us as Father, Son, and Holy Spirit.

THE ONE FLESH UNION OF MARRIAGE

Marriage is where the plurality of male and female becomes the unity of husband and wife. The oneness of marriage is referred to in the Bible as the one flesh union of husband and wife.

> Have you not read that he who created them from the beginning made them male and female, and said, "Therefore a man shall leave his father and his mother and hold fast to his wife, and they shall become one flesh"? So they are no longer two but one flesh. What therefore God has joined together, let not man separate. (Matthew 19:4–6)

It is clear from this passage that marriage is not defined by culture, a society, or by human beings at all, but by the very creation of God. Marriage is built into who we are as human beings in relationship to God. Whatever alterations a society may make of marriage, it will always eventually revert back to the reality God has given it. God has established marriage. There is no way to sustain marriage apart from honoring God's plan and will for marriage. In the end, all arrangements called marriage that are not the one flesh union of a man and woman will disintegrate and lead to the failure of the society that supports it. The will of God will prevail.

Shortly after God created man and woman in His image,

Adam recognized marriage at the creation of Eve:

> Then the man said, "This at last is bone of my bones and flesh of my flesh; she shall be called Woman, because she was taken out of Man. Therefore, a man shall leave his father and his mother and hold fast to his wife, and they shall become *one flesh*." (Genesis 2:23–24, *emphasis added*)

When a man and woman marry, their bond with their parents changes. A new and unique bond is created between husband and wife as they become one with each other in marriage. This *one flesh* union of marriage is difficult to describe or explain because there is nothing in our human experience to which it can be compared. More than anything, it is something like the bond between human beings and God. The one flesh union is different than the relationship between best friends or the bond between parents and children; it is not merely a feeling of closeness. Every spouse has time when he or she doesn't feel close to the other, but that is not the loss of the one flesh union. The one flesh union is a reality created by God, not by our mood; God establishes it through the husband and wife consummating their marriage.

Marriage is a good gift from God that gives human beings the delight of oneness that we could never create for ourselves. Even in the daily stresses of marriage, where this oneness seems to be missing or broken, this oneness remains, though hidden from us for the moment. At happy times in a marriage it may seem as though we can feel the oneness. This is the essence of romance. There are romantic moments when husband and

They are no longer two, but one flesh wife look into each other's eyes and realize how much they love each other after all those years. But even though expressed in such feelings, the one flesh union is more than the feeling itself.

This one flesh union within the bond of Christian love is affirmed in a Christian wedding ceremony, which is a covenant that is made between a man and a woman in the presence of God. This covenant is made publicly and promises faithfulness toward each other for a lifetime and benefit toward society. When a man and woman make this promise and consummate it, God then declares this to be marriage. Jesus affirmed marriage when he said, "They are no longer two but one flesh. What therefore God has joined together, let not man separate" (Matthew 19:6).

MARRIAGE AS MYSTERY

Marriage is a mystery! This is not meant to be humorous, as if to say that husband and wife are incomprehensible to each other. Rather it is to say that marriage is an incomprehensibly deeper reflection of more than is visible to either husband or wife. The Bible gives us one of its clearest descriptions of marriage in a letter from the apostle Paul to the Christians in the city of Ephesus in Asia Minor (Ephesians 5:21–33). Through Paul, God reveals part of the mystery of what it means to be husband and wife in marriage. We cannot completely explain a mystery, but we can learn and grow as each layer is revealed to us.

The mystery of God Himself is revealed most fully in the

New Testament with the coming of the Groom, Christ, for His bride, the Church. The apostle Paul helps us see the connection between the mystery of God and the mystery of marriage. After a detailed description in the fifth chapter of Ephesians of what it means to be a husband and a wife, Paul says that what he has really been writing about is not just the relationship between husband and wife, but, more important, the relationship between Jesus Christ and all believers. Paul concludes clearly,

> "This mystery [present in marriage] is profound, and I am saying that it refers to Christ and the Church." (Ephesians 5:32)

The word *mystery* is translated from the original Greek text (μυστήριον). Later, in the Roman world, Christians translated this same word *mystery* into Latin as *sacrament* (*sacramentum*). During the early years of the Lutheran Reformation, Martin Luther[3] used the Latin word *sacrament* to describe marriage.

> A sacrament[4] is a sacred sign of something spiritual, holy, heavenly, and eternal. . . . In the same way the estate of marriage is a sacrament. It is an outward and spiritual sign of the greatest, holiest, worthiest, and noblest thing that has ever existed or ever will exist: the union of the divine and human natures in Christ. The holy apostle Paul says that as man and wife united in the estate of matrimony are two in one flesh, so God

---

3. Luther later clarified the use of the word *sacrament*, but did not contradict what he wrote here.

4. Although Luther later clarified his use of the word *sacrament* for use in referring only to Baptism and the Lord's Supper, he continued to view marriage as the mystery referred to by St. Paul in Ephesians.

and man are united in the one person Christ, and so Christ and Christendom are one body. It is indeed a wonderful sacrament, as Paul says [Eph. 5:32] that the estate of marriage truly signifies such a great reality. Is it not a wonderful thing that God is man and that he gives himself to man and will be his, just as the husband gives himself to his wife and is hers?[5]

This *one flesh union* is a reflection of the *oneness* God creates between Himself and those who are wed to Him in love and trust through faith in Jesus Christ.

A metaphor from computer technology might help us understand the reflection of this mystery in marriage. Those familiar with the computer icon will know that when you click on an icon, it reveals the program to which it is attached. Marriage is such an icon that reveals God's program. When you "click" on marriage, you see the deeper reality of the relationship between Christ and those who are His people, wed to Him in love and trust. As Luther said above, "It is an outward and spiritual sign of the greatest, holiest, worthiest, and noblest thing that has ever existed or ever will exist."

To put it even more clearly: when you look more deeply into marriage, what you see is not just two people with a commitment to one another for life, but also a model of God's commitment to us for life. As man and woman have become one in marriage, so God has made us one with Himself in Jesus Christ. If there would ever be a divorcing of the marriage bond between God and us, it would not be due to unfaithfulness on

5.   James Atkinson, ed., *Luther's Works* (Philadelphia: Fortress, 1966), 44:10.

God's part but on ours. And if the marriage between God and His people continues, it is because of His faithfulness to us and His willingness to forgive our unfaithfulness. Someday we will join with Him in the wedding reception that goes on forever.

Marriage is a performance on earth of a heavenly reality lived out forever with God. Marriage is the sign, the mystery, and the icon that reveals to the faithful that we are one flesh with God for all eternity. This is why marriage cannot be whatever a society wants it to be. This is why marriage is only what God has made it to be. The singularity of male and female in the unity of the one flesh union of marriage bears witness to God as the maker of all things, even our salvation.

The conception of a child is the most natural result and the most wonderful evidence of the one flesh union that takes visual form. But not all conception and birth of a child bears witness to this unity. Among the greatest challenges before us today are the possibilities offered through reproductive technologies. Before we can know whether these reproductive technologies are compatible with what it means to be made in the image of God and bear witness to the one flesh union of marriage, we must assess the implications. For example, in marriage and procreation the two become one flesh, giving evidence of it in the birth of a child. But, with the use of donor sperm or egg or with surrogates who bear someone else's child within them, the one flesh is substituted for something else. Such substitution, however well intended, becomes an adulterous interruption of the one flesh union of marriage. It is adulterous even when husband and wife agree because one or both in agreement seek a child through someone outside their one flesh union to obtain what a marriage partner cannot provide. The fact that this occurs in a clinical setting of a doctor's office or hospital and not a neighbor's bedroom does not change the violation of the one flesh union of marriage. Couples who come to the realization that this is a violation can turn back to Christ, the Groom, who forgives our unfaithfulness and encourages us to live in renewed faith in His unfailing love.

As faithful people of God we do not have permission from God to redefine either marriage or reproduction for the sake of social needs or as an accommodation to the availability of reproductive technologies. Our children are visible signs of the one flesh union of marriage. This is not to say that all reproductive technologies are a violation of that oneness, but where participants outside the marriage are donors or surrogates, it is a violation. Adoption of a newborn or older child is not a violation of the one flesh union because it does not violate the intimacy of procreation. Here, the child is not brought into existence for the sake of our desire or expediency. Adoption is an act of hospitality to take in a child that has no parent able or willing to care for the child. Marriage is a mysterious proclamation of the Gospel in our world whether the world sees it or not. In the end, the mystery will be fulfilled for all to see. God has left evidence of His love and faithfulness to us in marriage, and our marriage must reflect the same love and faithfulness to the entire world.

Leading and following takes practice in dance and in marriage

Concluding Thoughts

My wife and I attend dances that sometimes have a mixer where dancers change partners in order to support a social network and introduce people to one another. It is hospitable to participate in mixers. I realize that some men or women do not have partners and this provides companionship and inclusion of those people. I do not participate in mixers very often because I love, most of all, to dance with my wife. Part of the problem with dancing with a stranger is that I find we don't know each other's style, patterns, or connections.

When I began working on leading, it took me a long time to experience the feel of what it means to actually *lead* and more time to understand the *connections* necessary in dancing with my wife as partner. Leading and following takes practice in dance and in marriage. My wife and I practice dancing daily at home as we have practiced marriage in our home all these years. We are still learning. It helps that we have chosen a strict tempo style of dancing and it helps that we have worked on patterns before working on styling. Marriage also requires a strict tempo of faithfulness and the work of commitment toward good patterns of living. As husbands we tend to step on a wife's toes when we are not attentive to what is going on between us. Developing a tempo of life together that allows practice in the "steps" of commitment, forgiveness, and renewal is a part of what it means to be one flesh. In order to make this happen, there needs to be agreement on the nature of marriage and what it means to *lead* and *follow*, even as Christ leads us and we follow Him in life.

may

MAY I LEAD, PLEASE?

After six months of weekly dance lessons, there came a day when I finally experienced what it really felt like to lead. From the beginning, our dance instructor had talked about how to lead, but the only things I heard at the time were the prohibitions: "Don't hold her hand so tightly that she can't turn. Don't use your hand on her back to push her. Don't tell her verbally what to do, let your body movement tell her." It was a surprise and it felt right to both my wife and to me the first time I was able to lead my wife full circle around the dance floor. Suddenly I was leading and she was following. The few steps we took blended beautifully into dance as dance should be. For at least a few moments, everything we had been working on became a

Learning how to lead and how not to lead requires teamwork, and we were becoming more of a team in dancing and in marriage.

blend of grace and skill. Prior to that, I had been depending on my wife to remind me what I had to do to lead, which of course meant that she was verbally leading me in leading her. Or, to put it simply, she was still leading me. To sustain us, I still needed a lot of practice in leading and she needed practice in following.

As I gradually learned how to lead on my own, our dancing improved dramatically. But even as I began to lead, it also became difficult for my wife to stop "being helpful" by leading me through the more difficult patterns of the dance at times. Even today we slip back into old patterns that disrupt the flow of the dance and I have to reminder her not to lead by asking rhetorically and winsomely, "May I lead, please?" She takes it well and we have both learned to laugh more since we began dancing than we ever did before. We laugh at ourselves and at each other's foibles. Some of it may be self-consciousness, but it beats getting angry at each other or yourself. Learning how to lead and how not to lead requires teamwork, and we were becoming more of a team in dancing and in marriage.

LEADING AND FOLLOWING IN MARRIAGE

In defining marriage in the Bible we have already said that both male and female are made in the image of God. A simple definition of what it means to be made in the image of God is to say that humans were created to be like God, at least in some ways. This is not to say that men and women were made like God in the same ways, as discussed in chapter 1. To differentiate the vocation God has given to a husband to lead and to a wife to follow in marriage the New Testament says, "I want you to understand that the head of every man is Christ, the head of a wife is her husband, and the head of Christ is God" (1 Corinthians 11:3).[1]

The authority to lead in marriage is given by God to the husband, just as it is the wife's calling from God to follow his lead.

There is an authority structure built into marriage that works to the benefit of both husband and wife. The authority to lead in marriage is given by God to the husband, just as it is the wife's calling from God to follow his lead. The meaning of the husband's leadership and of his wife's following is most clearly articulated in Ephesians:

> *Wives, submit to your own husbands, as to the Lord.* For the husband is the head of the wife even as Christ is the head of the church, His body, and is Himself its Savior. Now as the church submits to Christ, so also wives should submit in everything to their husbands.

> *Husbands, love your wives, as Christ loved the church and gave Himself up for her,* that He might sanctify her, having cleansed her by the washing of water with the word, so that He might present the church to Himself in

---

1. The verses that follow 1 Corinthians 11:3 address the application of this principle in terms of head coverings in church. Applications may vary with culture, but the principle remains intact, and each generation must wrestle with what that means in practice without denying the principle.

splendor, without spot or wrinkle or any such thing, that she might be holy and without blemish. In the same way husbands should love their wives as their own bodies. He who loves his wife loves himself. For no one ever hated his own flesh, but nourishes and cherishes it, just as Christ does the church, because we are members of His body. "Therefore a man shall leave his father and mother and hold fast to his wife, and the two shall become one flesh." This mystery is profound, and I am saying that it refers to Christ and the church. However, *let each one of you love his wife as himself, and let the wife see that she respects her husband.* (Ephesians 5:22–33, *emphasis added*)

A wife is to follow, that is, submit to her husband "as to the Lord," for her husband is the mask behind which God is leading them both in their one flesh union journey through life.[2]

In marriage, as in ballroom dancing, the husband must lead and the wife must follow, and apart from cultural changes in the acceptance or rejection of this ordering of marriage, it is the way God has made marriage to be. Marriage, as we understand from Ephesians 5:32, is a reflection of God's relationship between

- -

2. The marriage vows for a husband and wife are identical with the exception of a wife's declaration of her willing submission to her husband:

    Name of bridegroom, will you have this woman to be your wedded wife, to live together in the holy estate of matrimony as God ordained it? Will you nourish and cherish her as Christ loved His body, the Church, giving Himself up for her? Will you love, honor, and keep her in sickness and in health and, forsaking all others, remain united to her alone, so long as you both shall live?

    Name of bride, will you have this man to be your wedded husband, to live together in the holy estate of matrimony as God ordained it? Will you submit to him as the Church submits to Christ? Will you love, honor, and keep him in sickness and in health and, forsaking all others, remain united to him alone, so long as you both shall live? (Excerpt from *Lutheran Service Book Agenda* (c) 2006 Concordia Publishing House. All rights reserved.)

Himself and those who are His by faith in Jesus Christ. God the Father exhibits leadership in being in authority over the world; God the Son exhibits submission to the will of His Father on the cross; the Holy Spirit proceeds from the Father and the Son to bring about oneness between us and God by grace, through the faith He works in us.

ACCEPTING THE VOCATION TO LEAD

Leadership comes with authority, and authority prompts the vocation to lead. The husband taking the lead in marriage is a God-given vocation. It is a vocation that must always seek the well-being of their one flesh union as husband and wife. Taking the lead, the husband aims for the inclusion of his wife as a soul mate in order to enable them to live, love, and work well together in marriage.

Some men, by virtue of personality, are bold in leadership, while others are mild mannered, even passive, preferring to defer leadership to the wife. The personality of a husband's mother and father and the experiences of the marriage under which he was tutored provide the raw material with which he must work in learning to carry out his own vocation as husband. Whatever assets or liabilities this raw material may have provided, the shaping of his own leadership in marriage is at first often a matter of trial and error. A husband will model his father's leadership or reject it altogether in seeking to establish his own. From the mistakes he makes and from what he discovers about himself, he must make a conscious effort to make use of or leave behind those attitudes and behaviors from his inherited raw material, and affirm that which supports good leadership in his

Mistakes in leadership are inevitable . . .

own marriage. This may take years to accomplish and may never be the ideal he strives toward. Mistakes in leadership are inevitable and a husband's learning curve depends, in part, on his willingness and ability to recognize, admit, and learn from his mistakes as well as his successes.

A wife's vocation to follow her husband's lead is not easy because her own personality and the home in which she grew up also shapes her expectations of their relationship. She must examine her own experiences by observing her parents and attending to her reactions to her husband's errors in leadership to see how she must also change and grow to support him in his growth. Likewise, a husband must take into mind his wife's need for growth in learning to follow his lead. Her growth is his aim, just as his growth is hers. This is not to be construed as condescending for either of them unless one of them begin to focus more on the other's growth than on his or her own.

The model for learning is always Jesus Christ and His selfless giving in the face of outward resistance

The model for learning is always Jesus Christ and His selfless giving in the face of outward resistance. Christ was not intimidated by His vocation to lead the world back to His Father, nor did He submit to the cross out of weakness, but carried His cross with humility, faithfulness, and courage for the sake of his loved ones. Marriage calls for a unique kind of leadership and a unique kind of following. No successful leader micro-manages those he leads and no satisfied employee undermines a leader's honest attempts to lead. A husband's leadership must invite rather than coerce his wife's participation in marriage and a wife's following must be characterized by willingness rather than active or passive resistance. In a good marriage a husband's leadership is an expression of his love for his wife just as a wife's submission to her husband is an expression of her love for her husband, all of which results in their perfecting the dance of life together.

BEARING RESPONSIBILITY

In ballroom dancing, the woman is most often taking steps backward to the man's forward lead. Therefore, it is the responsibility of the man to protect and direct the woman because he can see where he is leading them both, and she cannot. However, whoever is taking forward steps is the one responsible for the safety of the other taking backward steps. Occasionally this means that as the man takes a few steps backward, the woman is leading for those few steps. It is the man, however, who is generally leading with the more frequent forward steps that enables them to circle the dance floor. He is therefore the one responsible for avoiding collisions with other dancers and for not putting his partner in danger.

In marriage, something similar occurs. The husband must protect his wife's personal security against physical danger, the injustice of others, and the threat of poverty. A husband's first and greatest task is to make his wife feel secure in their life together. A husband who refuses to provide for his family when he is fully able to do so, and sends his wife out in his place, is not taking the lead when he does so. This is not the case in those unique situations such as a husband's illness and/or disability or

A husband's first and greatest task is to make his wife feel secure in their life together.

a temporary set back in employment or his being called up to go off to war. As in dance, it may be that the woman will have to lead for a step or two as they carry out a measure of steps, but in the end the man returns to maintain his responsibility for her welfare, providing the necessary leadership for her to do her part in the marriage. She cannot follow him if he does not lead.

In those situations where it is not a refusal to work, but a necessity for such reasons just mentioned, the handing over of a husband's leadership to his wife may be seen as an extension of his own leadership, an assigned or delegated lead, in which his wife remains accountable to him even as she assumes the role of provider in behalf of their marriage. Husbands and wives need to discover each other's skills useful to their marriage and come to an agreed upon decision as to the wisest course to take, the husband bearing responsibility for them in the end, even for things he delegates to his wife. Unfortunately, many husbands have abdicated their responsibilities in marriage, expecting a wife to bear burdens he should be carrying. When this happens, a husband and wife may begin to resent each other, the wife becoming angry because her husband is not carrying his weight and the husband becoming angry because his wife, by his default, has taken over leadership of the marriage. Although a wife may be more competent than her husband to take the lead, leadership is not a choice they are given to make, but rather a vocation given by God to the husband to provide for his wife and family. Many wives often wish their husbands would take more leadership in their marriage even though they themselves find their own tendency to take charge difficult to give up to him.

For all the positive advances in women's rights in our society, many husbands are willing victims of the negative side of a feminism that demands husbands and wives share equal responsibility for leadership in a marriage. Those who promote gender neutrality claim that if there is any submission at all in marriage, it needs to be a two-way street. The wife should submit to the husband and the husband should submit to the wife. Some Christians quote Ephesians 5:21 to support this. The phrase, " . . . submitting to one another out of reverence for Christ," is taken out of context from that which actually states the reverse meaning. The verses that follow provide illustrations to show the meaning and nature of this submission. These illustrations are of husband-wife, child-parent relationships, and slave-master relationships.

Christians are to submit to one another wherever someone is in authority over them. In marriage, the wife is under the authority of her husband and therefore must submit to him. In parenting, the children are under the authority of their parents and must submit to them. In slavery, a slave is under the author-ity of a master and must submit to him. The example of slavery cited in Ephesians 6:5 is not an arrangement created by God as are marriage and child rearing, but is rather an example of how faithfulness through submission is possible wherever a Christian finds himself under authority, even unjust use of authority, which need not prevent a Christian from submitting faithfully to God in such a situation.

Someone may ask, "Is the wife's submission to her husband the same as the child's submission to a parent?" While in general terms submission does require one have control over another, this does not make the wife a child in relationship to her husband. What prevents this from happening is the way the husband exercises his leadership toward his wife and the nature of their relationship as one flesh. In relationship to his wife the husband exercises leadership in a way that builds the unique oneness and interdependence of marriage, not merely a dependent child-parent relationship that children necessarily outgrow as they mature. Similarly, the wife's submission to her husband is not the same as a slave's submission to his master. Slavery allows for no freedom or interdependence. The submission in marriage is not the forced submission of a slave to a master, but the development of an intimate relationship unique to the one flesh union that brings mutual benefit and delightful fulfillment to both in marriage.

AUTHORITY

Shifts in culture away from a wholesome understanding and respect for authority have added to the burden of reclaiming leadership in marriage. The effects of feminism on marriage over the past decades have undermined the concept of authority. Many can hardly allow themselves to pronounce the word *authority* without conveying the attitudes of suspicion and resentment. This negative association of the word *authority* with infringement on our freedoms is a residual of the 1960s. Occasionally it is still possible to find a car bearing the bumper sticker: "Question Authority!" We have come to equate all authority external to one's own as leading to authoritarianism that breeds oppression. The result of the assault on authority is that there is no longer any virtue left for many in the concept of authority, unless it be the authority of our own personal viewpoints or actions.

The 1970s was an introspective decade that gave rise to "encounter groups," a form of group therapy in which participants were urged to explore their feelings and learn to claim them as a foundation for their own authority. This appeal to *claiming your own authority* often generated resentment toward all external authority. In the light of decades of redefining authority as that which resides in the self, it is not surprising that there continues to be a discomfort for many with the suggestion that a husband should have authority over his wife. Even where husbands bear their own authority well in marriage, for those who lived through the 60s, 70s, and 80s, there often remains the lingering socially acceptable habit of outwardly rejecting the idea of a husband's authority for taking the lead in marriage. The irony is that what we are so conditioned to reject in principle, we often do in practice as those things which contribute to successful marriages.

The reason for the underlying persistence of authority in marriage, even against the grain of social movements that reject it, is not that men want to control women, but that authority is inherent in the nature of a husband and wife relationship. Cultures may vary in their transient attitudes toward marriage due to cultural and political movements, but eventually people revert to marriage as God made marriage to be simply because it works so well to build strong marriages. Strong marriages build

Strong marriages build strong families that in turn are the fundamental building blocks for a strong society.

strong families that in turn are the fundamental building blocks for a strong society. It is nature, not nurture alone, which makes marriage what it is.

Although in popular culture authority is perceived as one-dimensional, showing itself in abusive actions, the Bible presents the authority of God as multi-dimensional. The dimension God brings to the exercise of *authority* by the husband is his love for his wife. Authority and love are not mutually exclusive. God exercises authority in love over this world. Because we are made in the image of God, we see this multi-dimensional aspect reflected in our lives as parents as we *discipline* our children in *love*. The writer of Hebrews describes this as being the way God deals with us:

> My son, do not regard lightly the discipline of the Lord, nor be weary when reproved by Him. For the Lord disciplines the one He loves, and chastises every son whom He receives. (Hebrews 12:5–6)

Parents have the authority from God to discipline their children in love. This is something we need to remember when we suffer under God's hand knowing that, "for those who love God all things work together for good" (Romans 8:28). In marriage, the husband's authority over his wife is a mask for God's authority. Subsequently, both husband and wife wear the mask of parents who are in authority together over their children. This authority is tempered with God's warning to husbands and fathers, "Husbands, love your wives, and do not be harsh with them" and "Fathers, do not provoke your children, lest they become discouraged" (Colossians 3:19, 21).

The husband asserts his authority over his wife *in love* so that the wife's submission to his authority is not given with hesitancy, but with joy, as submission to Christ Himself. Paul declares: "Husbands love your wives, as Christ loved the church and gave Himself up for her" (Ephesians 5:25). Most clearly, God is saying, "Although you have been given the right to lead, when you exercise authority over your wife, do so in love!" A husband's love for his wife is to be as Christ's love for us in going as far as the cross for us. Although a husband is not perfect in exercising his authority and will often have reason to repent of its misuse, he does not allow his authority to become a continuing lifestyle of authoritarianism. The Letter to the Romans explains:

> How can we who died to sin still live in it? Do you not know that all of us who have been baptized into Christ Jesus were baptized into His death? We were buried therefore with Him by baptism into death, in order that, just as Christ was raised from the dead by the glory of the Father, we too might walk in newness of life. (Romans 6:2–4)

The Christian husband's sinful self has been crucified with Christ, so his vocation in marriage is to "walk in newness of life" and love his wife as Christ loved the Church and "gave Himself up for her." It is important for a husband to understand

"Husbands love your wives, as Christ loved the church and gave Himself up for her" (Ephesians 5:25).

Marriage, as our relationship with Jesus Christ, is about grace, freely given and undeserved.

that he is to give himself up for his wife. First, as Christ gave up His life for the Church yet did not give up His authority, so the husband's giving himself to his wife does not mean handing over his authority to her. Husbands are sometimes all too willing to hand over leadership to the wife and reenact the relationship of a child in submission to his mother. This can happen easily when a wife is more than willing to take charge of their life together. Second, a husband must know his wife well enough to not allow her to misuse the generosity of spirit in his self-giving. This means that a wife dare not take advantage of a husband's self-giving as simply a means to getting her way in times of disagreement. Third, some husbands claim that working long hours and being away from the wife more than usual is a way of sacrificing himself for her. In reality this often turns out to be the sacrificing of the wife for a husband's work.

The kind of sacrifice called for from a Christian husband is, first of all, the sacrifice of his self-centeredness. A husband's giving himself to his wife has more to do with him sacrificing his own self-interest for the good of the marriage relationship. As a husband of some four decades I can testify that there is nothing more difficult (or rewarding) than for a husband to strive to give up self-interest and to devote himself to the best interests of his wife. In fact, it is at least as difficult for a husband to give up self-interest as a way of loving his wife as it is for a wife to submit to her husband when his behavior or attitude is anything but deserving of her submission. The truth is that marriage is not about a wife deserving her husband's love or a husband deserving his wife's submission. Marriage, as our relationship with Jesus Christ, is about grace, freely given and undeserved.

Marriage is the arena of God's grace for a husband and wife lived out for the spouse. Marriages in which husband and wife bargain for advantage from one another are not marriages built on God's grace. It may happen that either husband or wife might fall into a bargaining marriage style that can be identified by an attitude such as, "He can go out with the guys tonight, but he owes me for time out when I want it" or "She owes me tonight for the flowers I brought home for her today." God's grace does not bargain; it gives freely to another for the benefit of the other and their unity in marriage. The cause of divorce is always, at the core of issues between them, the unwillingness of one or both to give freely of themselves to each other as God gives Himself to us. God's grace is God's undeserved love for sinful people. Husbands and wives must learn to love each other daily as sinful people seeking forgiveness from each other.

Although a man's vocation as a husband is to love his wife and bear the authority of his leadership for the benefit of their life together, this does not indicate that a wife is incapable of providing for her own physical needs, as if she couldn't manage without her husband. Indeed, wives left behind when their husbands go off to war must do this very thing. A wife is capable of bearing responsibility for her own life, but it is part of her submission to the Lord, through submission to her husband, to be willing to let him bear responsibility with and for her wherever possible. Her well-being is supported as he provides the emotional and physical security she needs to return love to her husband and to bring their children up in a family where they learn to love and trust in God through the example of their parents' marriage. It is no secret that many wives often sacrifice themselves for their husbands far more than their husbands do for their wives, but it is part of her submission to her husband to love him enough to help him grow into learning how to do the same for her. Husbands become better husbands when they learn to do this. Wives enable husbands to learn this when they willingly submit to their own husbands.

The worst thing a husband can do is abuse his authority by abusing his wife. A wife's submission to her husband ought to never be understood as a requirement to submit to physical abuse, merciless dominance, or heartless authoritarianism. The Word of God does not permit abuse when it urges, "Wives, submit to your husbands." This is not to give permission to a wife to divorce her husband for his occasional outbursts anymore than it is for him to divorce her for her times of bad temper and absence of submission. We must all take some minor abuse from each other as sinful human beings, but when the safety of wife and children are at stake under an abusive husband, necessary and immediate intervention should be sought by the police, a marriage counselor, and the pastor.

CONCLUSION

We have tried to define what it means for a husband to lead and a wife to follow in the dance of marriage. We have spoken of the husband's leadership in terms of his authority to lead in marriage. The claim was also made that the husband's authority in marriage is established by God and not by cultural norms, just as marriage itself is not whatever we wish it to be, but is what God has made it to be. We have also made a case for the fact that a husband's authority requires him to lead and love for the mutual benefit of his marriage and family. And we have tried to show that the line of authority in marriage originates and flows from God through the husband in relationship to the wife, and through husband and wife together in relationship to their children. We might also view this from the point of view of the one in submission. Children look to their parents, as the wife looks to the husband, as the husband looks to God, for leadership.

Finally, we might also think of leadership in marriage in the wider and narrower sense. In the wider sense, the husband is responsible to God for his leadership as husband in the marriage. In the narrower sense, both husband and wife bear responsibility together for much of daily decision-making that affects their marriage to the end that what is decided is compatible with what God has made marriage to be for them. Decision-making is not easy when the strong will of husband and wife are in conflict. In the next chapter we will see how difficult it is for the husband to lead and the wife to follow when they find themselves in the conflicts of daily living. It is only through the sacrifice of self and mutual forgiveness that daily conflicts can be turned into moments of God's grace at work in their marriage.

it's always

It's Always the Man's Fault

Rule number one for the man in ballroom dancing is: "When the woman makes the wrong move in a dance pattern, it's the man's fault." I was certain that our instructor concealed a smile as he said this. In all honesty, I didn't believe it and laughed it off. Surely no red-blooded American male is going to assume he is at fault when his wife does something wrong, but it became very clear that in ballroom dancing the rule was to be taken seriously—at least most of the time. I thought taking the blame for my wife's faults in dancing was merely a nice way of saying, "Give your wife the benefit of the doubt." So, in order to be congenial during lessons, I jokingly repeated the rule and accepted blame whenever something went wrong in our danc-

Marriage as an opportunity for mutual personal growth is a unique and rich experience.

ing. As I soon learned, ninety-nine percent of the time, when my wife didn't follow my lead, it was because I did not lead properly. As leader, I was nearly always the one at fault.

Determining fault in order to correct a problem is a little less clear in marriage than it is in dancing. Throughout our marriage, when one of us had a complaint, my wife and I had almost always talked out our problems openly, spending many hours over the years analyzing whatever problems there were between us in the hope that we might deal with them constructively the next time they appeared. It was a pattern we knew we needed to maintain, especially when it was difficult to do at times. Even if the origin of the problem arose solely from one or the other, we both knew that by the time we had argued it out, both of us had contributed to the worsening of the problem. Sometimes our problem was resolved in civilized discussion, but there were times we argued heatedly into the night, long after we should have been asleep, yet nearly always resolving the issue to our mutual satisfaction in the end. We had both learned that the problem we faced in our relationship was not his or her problem, but our problem. Some wise observer had said to us early in our marriage that if one person had a problem in the marriage, then both had a problem that needed to be faced. As our marriage matured we found it saved time to honestly admit our faults to each other early and genuinely forgive each other so that we could move on to a solution to the problem at hand.

Because we had established this pattern in our marriage, in dance lessons it was no big deal for me to point out my wife's fault or for her to point out my improper lead. We began to be able to quickly face our own and each other's liabilities as well as assets in ballroom dancing. And, yes, there are times when the man may lead properly and the woman still makes the wrong move. Even our instructors admitted that would continue to happen from time to time. But the truth of it is that in dancing, my wife's not following my lead really was my fault most of the time. If I did not communicate clearly what I expected of her with my "frame" or our "connections," she would not know how to follow my lead even if she wanted to do so. Dancing continued to emerge as a metaphor for marriage. If either of us could not communicate clearly what we needed in our marriage, how could the other know how to respond to it?

It is not unusual for one partner in marriage to be clear about personal needs and the other not. This may be the result of upbringing or it simply may be differences in personality or both. Some people know themselves and their needs well and others don't have a clue and struggle to discover them. Some people are needy, but don't know how to get those needs met constructively in marriage. Marriage as an opportunity for mutual personal growth is a unique and rich experience. For example, intimacy to a man is generally understood as physical in nature whereas to a woman intimacy is first of all relational. Intimacy is both physical and relational and can only really be learned in marriage. The exciting thing about marriage is that there is opportunity to learn something new about yourself and your spouse throughout a lifetime of marriage.

There are times when conflicts simply cannot be resolved and you learn to live without their complete resolution. In dancing, when we forget or are under stress from the day's events, we both tend to tighten our grip on each other, causing us problems in both leading and following. Likewise, over the years of marriage it becomes clear that some things will never change and each of us must learn to live with some fault in the other that will not go away. In time, with a sense of humor, couples can learn to laugh at these faults when they are not so serious that they damage the marriage. The same is true when we are dancing and everything seems to be going wrong. Laughing at oneself and *agreed upon* laughter at each other does relieve the tension. There are rare occasions when we simply have had to say, "This is not our night for dancing!" and leave the dance floor. Tomorrow is another day.

Some faults in dancing, as in marriage, are not fundamental faults in our ability to dance or maintain the marriage, but are mysteriously part of the flow of life that itself falls short of perfection. When there is no apparent solution to an ongoing problem in marriage, there is always the love of God and the forgiveness of sins that reflects itself in our love and forgiveness toward each other. It is important to remind each other of that.

FACING UP TO PROBLEMS

In dancing, problems arise due to both external environment and internal conflicts. I remember the first time my wife and I attended a dance outside the safe environment of our dance studio. At the studio, everyone was a learner and danced as poorly as we did or remembered a time when they were learning and were therefore generous toward our faults. There were people there who had had only one or two lessons before their first dance and there were others who had decades of dance experience and were still attending studio dances for reasons of their own. But in the world of ballroom dance, where people came to enjoy a night of dancing, survival on the dance floor was a tangle of surprises for us at every turn. The environment on the dance floor can seem almost hostile at first. Barely would we begin a few steps when someone would move in front of us causing us mentally to stumble in our novice attempts to do things right. After a few tries at joining the crowds we sat out the next dance; once or twice we went home discouraged.

The first thing I had to learn in ballroom dancing is that public dancing is like driving on the freeway in rush hour. Because I love driving and was once given the compliment (in my view at least) that I drive like a New York cabby, this metaphor helped me get perspective on dancing. You have to learn how to use the brakes as well as the accelerator and, unlike a New York cabby, you have to be patient with others as well as with yourself. There are rules of the ballroom, as there are rules of the road, and as in rush hour traffic not everyone either knows or follows them.

In ballroom dancing the movement of experienced dancers is around the outside of the dance floor. The center of the dance floor is reserved for those not yet able to manage the open road. These "insiders" are expected to dance in the center where it is safe and they are less likely to cause an accident. Safety, as well as enjoyment, is planned! I did not feel safe the first time we undertook to move into the mainstream of traffic on the dance

> Marriage is not always rational, but choosing how and when to argue is something worth working toward.

floor. Dancers faster and more skilled than we came rushing up behind us just as in rush hour traffic. If they were skilled and thoughtful, they would miss us. If not, they would nudge by causing a minor fender-bender as if to say, "Move it, buddy!" But nearly all were polite and apologetic. These same people seated at tables between dances were congenial and supportive of us as novices and recalled their own early years of learning to dance.

Marriage can also be chaotic at times. Learning the rules of marriage early in life together can save the day later on. Mutually agreed upon rules that define the boundaries of a disagreement such as "While arguing, neither of us will walk out on the other" or "In disagreements we will work at not attacking the other person but stay on the issue" or "If the timing for dealing with a disagreement is not good, we will together set another time to discuss it." Marriage is not always rational, but choosing how and when to argue is something worth working toward. Rush hour traffic in the home need not always be chaotic.

Conflict not only arises from external environment but also from internal personal conflicts. Just as there may be environmental problems with the music, other dancers, or the surface of the dance floor, there are also the internal realities of tiredness, lack of confidence, loss of concentration, and simply forgetting techniques of how to lead or how to follow. I know myself well enough to recognize that there are times I feel like dancing and times I don't. If my mind is not in favor of dancing, things quickly turn against me as the evening progresses. I am less patient with myself, with my wife, and with other dancers. But if I go dancing with a light-heartedness and the prospect of having fun, my dancing may or may

Conflict in marriage arises out of both environmental and internal factors . . .

not be the best that night, but it doesn't matter all that much. I know that eventually I will improve as the evening progresses or at a future dance.

Attitude is a large part of what makes dancing go well. I am a competitive person in work or play, but my greatest competitor is myself, and I am as goal oriented toward dancing as I am toward my work. Dancing is both work and play. My wife is also competitive and finds the challenge of her goal orientation is the challenge of concentrating on technique while still being attentive to my lead. Concentration on what's happening is as essential in dancing as it is in marriage.

Conflict in marriage arises out of both environmental and internal factors as well. Although God has clearly designed marriage as He means for it to be lived, the cultural influences and environment constantly challenge God's design. For example, sexuality intended by God for marriage alone is offered to us in a supermarket variety of opportunities both premaritally and extramaritally. We live in an environment of premarital and extramarital sexual activity supported by *freedom of choice* agencies and institutions that encourage sexual expression inhibited only by the warning to take precautions to avoid sexually transmitted disease and pregnancy, as if the latter was the equivalent evil of the former. The environment in sex

In marriage we are needy for what we find in each other.

education in public schools is to advise abstinence until a child is *of age*; the implication being that maturity, not morality, is the issue. Waiting for sex until marriage is believed to be unrealistic. Premarital and extramarital sex as portrayed on television is accepted as the norm for life.

Equal to environmental threats to growth in marriage are the internal conflicts that continue unresolved throughout a marriage. None of us comes into a marriage with perfectly well-adjusted lives. All of us exhibit some dysfunctional patterns of behavior at times. Ironically, we are often drawn together as much by what is wrong with us as we are by what is right with us. As much as these individual patterns of behavior may threaten a marriage, they can also provide opportunity for mutual growth and healing. In marriage we are needy for what we find in each other. Some of that neediness is healthy and some is not, but marriage gives us opportunity to mature together. This *becoming one flesh*, called marriage, draws us into each other to form a new person between us. We don't lose our individuality. We become who God intended us to become by being one with each other. Fulfillment of the individual is found in the giving of oneself to the other in marriage where we live for each other as much as we do for ourselves. This bond of marriage is a reflection of the bond between Christ and the Church. That bond between Christ and the Church makes us one, and that oneness is reflected in our marriage.

As inattentiveness in ballroom dancing can lead to a breakdown of the dance, so inattentiveness in marriage can lead to a breakdown of the relationship. If left unattended to, the breakdown in relationship can lead to serious problems and possibly divorce and the breaking of the one flesh union of marriage. My wife and I began ballroom dance lessons in the summer, and we were less harried by schedules and pressures than in the winter months. As a result, we spent much of the summer practicing the basic steps we learned early in our lessons. We spent an hour each day in our home laboring over the things we had been taught. My wife and I recall with amusement how hard it was to learn the basics of the cha-cha. The hardest thing about this dance is the constant change in direction at a high rate of speed. The early years of marriage also move at a high rate of speed, and if we don't work at practicing the right things in the beginning, the marriage becomes more burdensome in later years until we consciously take action to correct it. Couples I have counseled after a divorce often say that things were not good from the beginning, but they were never attended to at the time or even later.

. . . inattentiveness in marriage can lead to a breakdown of the relationship

One of the goals of ballroom dancing is for the man to make the woman look good on the dance floor. He may be doing the harder work of leading, but he is not to be the object of notice as much as his partner. The man sets the stage for the woman to dance well. In marriage, this means the husband's love for his wife is aimed at her happiness and fulfillment. In an argument between husband and wife a lot of energy is spent in each trying to make oneself look good and the other bad. In marriage a husband needs to work at meeting his wife's need for security, her need for his selfless love, and her need for spiritual growth. If he is able to do this, the reciprocal response of love and faithfulness also will fulfill a husband's needs. It is the husband's job to enable his wife to love him so that there is fulfillment in the one flesh of marriage for both of them.

Some people in the dance of life just don't get it. As part of my clinical training for hospital chaplaincy, along with other trainees I participated in what often turned into the equivalent of group therapy sessions. The aim of these sessions was to get to know and understand your own strengths and weaknesses in relating to people so that we could be more helpful and effective as hospital chaplains. We would eventually provide pastoral care to dying patients and their families, those experiencing new traumatic disabilities and a variety of other serious illnesses in which we would sometimes discover patients and personalities that were not easy to care for. As we practiced and revealed our own personalities to each other in the group sessions, thereby simulating patient interaction, we worked at responding openly and honestly to one another. One trainee, who invited honesty from others, had a habit of using the received self-disclosure of others as a way of manipulating them in future sessions. She would invite each of us to be open and honest about our weaknesses and use them against us whenever she felt "threatened" in the sessions. This can also happen in marriage. In time, couples get to know the "soft" or vulnerable spots in each other's personality and either intentionally or unintentionally target these in heated arguments. It is a serious, but not uncommon, way of hurting the other person.

Arguing Badly and Arguing Well

My wife and I didn't have our first argument until we had been married almost three years. Because things had been going so well in our marriage and because we were both open to learn more about our marriage, we dared to enroll in a yearlong marriage enrichment program with nine other couples. Our first real argument took place shortly after becoming participants in the enrichment course. My wife took a stand on something we disagreed about and wouldn't budge. I have no idea any more what it was we disagreed about, but she felt the need to take a stand and she did. From that moment on we argued with vigor and tenacity, not often, but with pizzazz when we did so. We might say that it was in the marriage enrichment course that we learned to disagree and argue well. That sounds strange, but had we not learned to argue well I suspect a great deal of resentment would have built up over the years and perhaps strained the relationship beyond repair.

Couples who never argue at all, beware! During the first three years of our marriage we believed rightly that we had a good marriage, and someone observing us in those days might have quoted the proverb: "If it ain't broken, don't fix it." Our marriage wasn't broken, but we tried to fix it anyway. Our marriage needed maturity and, for us, apparently argumentation seemed the way of reaching it. Because we learned to argue our differences in the context of this enrichment program we learned to argue constructively, at least much of the time. It took years to perfect a "good argument" yet even now we slip back into "bad arguments" once in a while. In either case, we contin-

There are times to talk about problems and times not to talk about them.

ued to learn to argue long enough to resolve an issue to the satisfaction of both of us. And of course, reconciliation after an argument can lead to passion that also heals.

In fact, every couple has had the experience of one partner picking a fight with the other as a means of getting closer to the other. This can work sometimes, but it can also backfire and make the distance greater between them. A better way to get closer to each other is to talk and face up to problems together before they reach the point of an argument. The question of when to talk is essential. There are times to talk about problems and times not to talk about them. When we felt pressures building up inside us toward the other, we learned to agree to a time later in the day when we could talk. As that time arrived we found that the frustration had dissipated and it was easier to talk about the issue. Postponing problem solving can be good if the time set to face up to it is not cancelled or postponed again.

As time went on we learned to argue in half the time by eliminating the habit of playing "old tapes." "Old Tapes" are those things we do and say that have little if anything to do with the argument at hand but are dragged in from leftover unresolved issues of previous arguments or leftover issues from life before marriage. Each of us brings to the marriage the patterns in which we were raised. Not only do we sometimes mimic our parent's way of arguing, but we also bring with us well-honed weapons for defense in time of war. Some learn to wear the enemy down with silence. Others attack from behind with low blows that hurt and weaken the enemy. Arguments can unleash much that is irrelevant to the issue at hand and confuse points of argument. Every couple has sometimes argued long and hard only to look at each other exhausted and ask, "What was the issue we were arguing about, anyway?" As already mentioned, sometimes people just need to argue as a means of getting closer to each other than they were before. My wife and I both thought there ought to be a better way to get close to each other, but we also agreed that arguing is better than ignoring each other or going our separate ways. When we argued badly, we tried to reassure each other that despite some relapses in this argument, we were both still working on overcoming those things we did that interfered with our arguing constructively.

The husband's leadership is exercised, in part, by not allowing his wife to provoke him into an argument. He will not be able to prevent her attack, but how he responds to it is up to him. Why might a wife provoke an argument? Because she is tired, frustrated, angry, feeling neglected, lonely, or any number of other feelings or circumstances. I am not here speaking of wives whose continuous conversation is a litany of complaints, but of those times when tranquility is pierced by a wife's cry of desperation unjustly taken out on her husband. Responding to her in defensive anger does not help. A wife's invitation to argue may lead to greater distance between husband and wife, thereby accomplishing the opposite of her need to be cared for and loved.

In taking the lead in a provocative argument a husband does well to keep quiet and listen much of the time, not feeding the frenzy. What a wife wants more than anything from her

If we are to argue and complain in a marriage, let us do it well and not badly.

husband is a listening ear that hears her frustrations that may be unclear even to herself. It is not necessary that a husband understand everything that is going on as she pours out her complaint, but it is necessary that he listen patiently until she is finished. This is one of his crosses to bear. She will know whether he is listening to her in spirit. A husband may have difficulty keeping his silence when his wife poses her complaint in the form of accusations and blame targeting him when the source of her frustration is clearly someone or something else. He is wise to learn the difference between her need for support at such times and the legitimacy of her complaint against him. The wise husband, as leader, will not provoke his wife into greater anger or frustration. His reluctance to do this ought not be due to his fear of her anger, but for her well-being. He needs to maintain his leadership by helping her benefit by their relationship and his support.

If we are to argue and complain in a marriage, let us do it well and not badly. In disciplined philosophical debate the first rule is, "Don't attack the person; address the issue itself." Stay clear of personal attacks and target the issue together. Personal attacks not only delay and prevent finding a solution to the problem, but they also cause hurt, resentment, and guilt in people who otherwise love and care about each other. One of the most devastating and provocative things to do in a marital disagreement is to begin a sentence with, "You always . . ." or "You never . . ." Even if it is true that a husband or wife "always" or "never" does or says this or that, it contaminates a good argument with irrelevant accusations. A better time to talk about what either person "always" or "never" does is after the issue-oriented argument is resolved and both have confessed their wrong(s) to the other and each has forgiven the other. When the argument and hostile feelings are over, an analysis of how we argue with each other is an appropriate learning experience.

Of course, the reality is that marital disagreements are often filled with legitimate complaints about the other person. In this case, each at least needs to be honest and not exaggerate the other's faults, realizing that no one changes under pressure. In marriage we change, if we are willing to change at all, when others tell us things about ourselves in love, with the aim of helping the relationship we have with that person. Arguing well is an art that needs to be practiced and learned over time, and even when we are able to do so, there is always the need for mutual confession and absolution. Few good arguments are without some injury given or received and so the Lord speaks of "bearing with one another and, if one has a complaint against another, forgiving each other" (Colossians 3:13).

CONFESSING AND FORGIVING

If I ever allow myself to think that the need for confessing one's sins is an infrequent necessity, I need only think of my own marriage. Having been joyfully married for nearly forty years to a woman I dearly love, disagreement has not been a predomi-nate characteristic of our relationship. However, there have always been those regretful moments in which each of us said things we ought not to have said and held anger against the other when it should have been left behind sooner. Fortunately,

Marriage is about new beginnings every day.

my wife taught me the meaning of forgiveness in our marriage. At the conclusion of one of our first arguments, I recall apologizing to my wife for being insensitive and unwilling to hear what she was saying and, as a result, with considerable grace she replied, "I forgive you." Her boldness in actually speaking those words made an impact on me and I wondered if I was prepared to receive them, for it occurred to me that my repentance might not have been as genuine a response as it may have seemed. I was suddenly aware that I may have apologized merely to end the disagreeable experience rather than to actually admit I had done wrong or had sinned against her. That moment of her gracious forgiveness, remembered and repeated often over our marriage, still amazes me as being unduly generous and accepting of me as one who never seems to learn.

I was not prepared for her absolution and it caught me off guard. It is one thing to admit your fault, even your sin, and quite another for someone to confirm your confession as necessary and then to repay it with forgiveness. The pronouncement of forgiveness shakes the very foundations of our imperfect lives. Forgiveness both acknowledges that we are right to confess our sins and takes control of us so that we are renewed for a new beginning in Christ. Marriage is about new beginnings every day. Those bogged down in old resentments over the years may not know what this means from experience. The ways to find out is to conclude your next argument with your confession of wrongs (sins) against your husband or wife regarding the things you know you should not have said and then ask for forgiveness. It may take time for your husband or wife to respond verbally and sometimes it comes in attitude if not in words. Ultimately, words of forgiveness need to be spoken when each person is ready to speak them. One way to set the stage for the possibility of such confession and reconciliation is to look into each other's eyes while dancing and say, "I love you!" All this comes from God who loves us, forgives us, and reconciles us to Himself so that we might live in peace and joy with Him. Marriage is where He reminds us of this.

the sensuality

THE SENSUALITY OF
DANCE AND MARRIAGE

My first school dance was in seventh grade. I remember wearing a white sport jacket, dark pants, and a pink carnation in my lapel. That's how young men dressed for dances in the early 1950s and I felt so grown up in doing so. The woman across the street from where we lived ran a dance school in her home. My parents signed me up for lessons, no doubt in the hope that I would learn to enjoy dancing as much as they did, but my experience was a disaster. In a class of five, I was the only 13-year-old, the rest being primarily 8- to 10-year-olds. I was humiliated and refused to return for my second lesson.

of dance...

Nevertheless, untutored, I was determined to attend my first junior high dance. The excitement of anticipating the event was diminished only by my knowledge that I had no idea how to dance.

After the dance studio disaster, in preparation for my first dance that night, my Mom tried to teach me the box step, but that only gave rise to fears of my stepping all over my partner's feet. However, I never did step on one toe because I never danced that night. As we arrived, the guys gathered on one side of the gymnasium and the girls on the other. After what seemed an eternity of trying to get up enough courage to walk over and ask a girl to dance, I took the coward's way out and poked the guy next to me. Glad for the diversion, all the guys began poking and chasing each other around the gym. That's what guys did when they felt self-conscious and wanted go have a good time without girls. The girls eventually gave up in disgust and began dancing with each other.

The appeal of actually dancing with a girl took another year to appreciate, but by then my developing libido was so strong I was afraid to get close to a girl for fear of embarrassing results. By the end of high school I had begun to mature enough to learn to manage both my emotions and my sensual nature. It was my best friend's girlfriend that taught both him and me how to dance. That was safe, and we could dance together without my daring to think of her as anything other than my best friend's girl. While my best friend was dating her, she and I also became best friends. The three of us went to dances together. It was in this experience of friendship that I learned to enjoy dancing for its own sake, even though it would take nearly fifty years before attempting dance lessons again.

Sexual Desire and Sensuality[1]

Sexual desire as sensuality is part of God's design for human beings, but God intends that a man and woman wait until marriage to fully explore their own sensuality and have sexual intercourse. My wife and I recently had dinner at a nice restaurant and heard two men at the next table comparing their sexual encounters aloud. One said to the other, "I lived with Marie for a year to see if we were sexually compatible, but found out we were not, so we split." I wanted to interrupt and say, "You've got it backward. You have to work at the relationship in the commitment of marriage for years before sensuality and sexual intercourse fully mature as an expression of the relationship."

Cultural behaviors and attitudes vary in time and place, giving approval or disapproval to sexual intimacy and intercourse before marriage, but God's people are called to be faithful to God in trusting that He put marriage before these for a reason. The Word of God affirms our sensuality saying, "If anyone thinks that he is not behaving properly toward his betrothed,[2] if his passions are strong, and it has to be, let him do as he wishes: let them marry" (1 Corinthians 7:36). "Let marriage be held in honor among all, and let the marriage bed be undefiled, for God will judge the sexually immoral and adulterous" (Hebrews 13:4). Marriage and family is the foundation

----

1. Song of Solomon 7, as the Word of God, speaks sensually of a man's love for a woman as metaphor for God's love for His beloved, the people of God.

2. Betrothal did not include the right to sexual intercourse.

for community that creates a society and that teaches faithfulness to God in all things.

Fulfillment of sexual desire ultimately takes place rightly in sexual intercourse in marriage. As sexual desire comes to life in us long before we are ready for marriage, so sensuality as an expression of that desire can be legitimate without leading to what must be reserved for marriage. For example, I can remember the sensuality of the moment I first summoned the courage to hold the hand of a girl I liked. The fact that this would not be a sensual experience for many today only testifies to the fact that taking one thing at a time in the right order can make sensuality a delight all along the way to and throughout marriage. Even today, while on a long walk, my wife and I still delight in holding hands as a physical expression of our love and desire for each other.

When my wife and I began ballroom dance lessons, we simply wanted to learn social dancing. I had just retired. The pressures of work were diminished and I began to discover my wife as the center of my life more than ever. We started dancing by learning the waltz. As close as we had always been, it was not long into our lessons that I realized how much dancing together allowed us to look into each other's eyes, something I hadn't done intentionally for a while. I was overwhelmed at the delight in my wife's eyes and I realized with great emotion how much I loved her and recalled

Marriage and family is the foundation for community that creates a society and that teaches faithfulness to God in all things.

the Song of Solomon, "You have captivated my heart with one glance of your eyes" (Song of Solomon 4:9b). The music, the dance, and my wife's love poured into my heart. This was a sensuality that no one else could see but us. In this outwardly modest, but definitely sensual experience of dance with the woman I have always loved, there seemed to be the sign of everything God intended for us in marriage. Wholesome sensuality may reach heights "only with your wife in the privacy of the bedroom," but it can also be found more modestly on the dance floor. When asked to write a testimonial for the dance studio website, I wrote:

Although we have always been close and had a wonderful marriage, our dancing together has been an experience of falling in love with each other all over again.

WHOLESOME SENSUALITY

Although the primary emphasis at the studio we attended was on competitive dance, my wife and I neither desired nor conceded to our instructors, who were urging us to sign up for ballroom dance competition. The dramatic movement and patterns, the costumes and dresses, the lavish makeup, the jewelry, and the glitz of it all did not appeal to us personally and yet we admired the skill and grace of those who did competitive dancing. Our admiration for this came slowly. After seeing an advanced student-couple perform a rumba exhibition,[3] the response of my wife and me as we looked at each

----

3.   An exhibition, unlike a competition, allows a couple to work toward excellence in a dance and share it before other dance students in the studio. It allows a couple to do more than they could on a crowded public dance floor.

other was, "Never will I dance that way with anyone but you," and joked, "Even then we might have to resort to the bedroom." Actually, we discovered the dancers to be a husband-wife couple and because we thought they danced so beautifully together, we told them so. Unprompted, the wife of the couple sheepishly revealed that her thoughts were much like our own as she admitted, "I could never dance like this with anyone but my husband." What we saw in this husband and wife couple was genuine, wholesome, appropriate sensuality.

As we observed more professional dancers, we concluded that many couples with no romantic connections danced almost as beautifully together, mimicking the intimacy and sensuality of those who, like this married couple, did love each other. Competition ballroom dancing is theater, and theater portrays life. The drama, the costumes, the makeup, the kind of dance itself, makes competitive ballroom dance theater. Theater has the potential to restore sensuality to its rightful place in marriage or to exploit sensuality for its own sake. If ballroom dancing can communicate wholesome sensuality such as that which exists between husband and wife, it can then serve as a sign of where wholesome sensuality can be found: in marriage. It became clear to us that those we met in the studio, instructors and students alike, had a high ethical view that allowed little room for unwholesome sensuality in dance.

As difficult as it is to define wholesome sensuality, it hardly seems necessary to define unwholesome sensuality today. Unwholesome sensuality is clearly recognized in pornography, exploitive exhibitionism on television, public theater that panders to deviant sexuality, and lifestyles that reject marriage as the place where God intends fulfillment of sensuality. It is important to realize, however, that an unwholesome sensuality can also be found in marriage. When the sensual in marriage centers on self-gratification more than on the mutual delight in the one flesh unity of two-become-one, this becomes an unwholesome sensuality. When a husband's desire overrides respect for his wife and her needs, this becomes an unwholesome sensuality. When desire is focused on conquest or control, this becomes unwholesome sensuality. A husband's bargaining for sex with his wife becomes unwholesome, at times mimicking that of a child begging for candy. A husband's becoming a husband in their relationship begins with his ability to love his wife freely without demanding sexual reward. A husband who demands of his wife her "duty" to have sex stands far from the wholesome sensuality God calls for from those who are one in Christ.

From Sexual Desire to Relationship

In young newlyweds sexual desire begins in serving its own interests and there is pleasure in sensuality for its own sake. However, as a marriage matures sexual desire is fed by the deepening relationship, which in turn renews sensuality even into old age. Marriage is about *making love* and not just about *having sex*! The meaning of *making love* is that husband and wife are *working* at winning each other over toward deepening their relationship. Making love may include sexual intercourse, depending on the mutual decision to either postpone or continue the passion of the moment appropriate to the situation, for making love always aims at the building of their love and unity. In contrast, the connotation of having sex is that of two people carrying out a biological function that has little to do with relational meaning or the need for personal intimacy. It is an expression invented by those who have reduced sexual desire to being an end in itself. The expression *having sex* leaves little room for a distinction between being involved sexually with prostitute or spouse.

The frequency and quality of sexual desire cyclically decreases and increases throughout the lifetime of a marriage. When a newly married couple is young, before children arrive and there are few demands made upon on them in life, sexual desire seems to be a an ever-flowing river without rapids or waterfall, but as children come along and responsibilities at work increase, the journey downstream becomes exhausting and frustrating, in turn, affecting sexual desire as never before. As a marriage ages, unresolved conflicts between husband and wife over the years can diminish a couple's sexual desire for each other. In marriage the sexual desire in both husband and wife shifts through highs and lows according to circumstances and life changes.

Every married couple knows how stress affects sexual desire. Conflict and stress can increase the emotional distance between husband and wife. When sufficient distancing occurs, a spouse may eventually seek multiple activities outside the home that distract from the marriage, sexual satisfaction in flirtatious, emotionally adulterous relationships, or pornography (if not adultery itself). But these substitutes for devotion to the spouse threaten, damage, and even destroy a relationship between husband and wife. Sexual desire becomes self-serving and the satisfaction found in their relationship with each other suffers. Sexual desire in good marriages may unfortunately be diminished by mental illness such as depression or even the medications to treat it. Fortunately, there are also med-

Conflict and stress can increase the emotional distance between husband and wife.

ications to increase sexual desire and to assist in overcoming problems such as erectile dysfunction and loss of libido. In the end, the medicine that heals all wounds in a marriage is the forgiveness of sins and the love husband and wife have for God that spills over into love for the other where the relationship can deepen in a sensuality that is tender and fulfilling in itself.

Sensuality can grow even through times of illness, hardship, and aging. The trauma of menopause, an empty nest, the death of a family member, or the disability of a spouse can affect husband and wife so that the sexual desire that once flowed so easily may no longer seem to flow at all. Sexual desire can wane under the weight of grief, personal struggles, or the demands of other people and circumstances. As couples grow older the stress of being part of the *sandwich generation*, caught between the needs of their children and those of their aging parents can also diminish sexual desire. As difficult as these things may be, this is an opportunity for couples to turn to each other for greater intimacy and support, even when they are not able to give way to sexual intercourse as they have in the past. It is necessary for a couple to take time for each other rather than avoiding each other and allowing their relationship

> . . . a husband and wife need to take time for each other . . .

to get buried beneath resentment and frustration.

Romantics may believe that love is a feeling and that, once lost, that feeling cannot be recovered, but husbands and wives who have remained faithful to each other and have worked at making their marriage successful know that love is a calculated, intentional commitment between them that rewards them with deeper meaning as hardship piles on. The "end" toward which all feeling and calculation and all sensuality and sexual desire aims for in marriage is the building of that deepened, satisfying relationship that reflects the deeper, satisfying relationship between God and each of them.

It was only after many years that I came to realize that it was with great effort that my wife responded affirmatively to my last-minute phone calls to her to have lunch with me during my busy work day. I am thankful she did. It required of her at the time that she drop whatever she was happily doing, quickly find a babysitter, and drive downtown to meet me for lunch. These were often important lunch times together because they allowed us to nurture our relationship in ways we would otherwise never have had time to do with the children around.

When everyone else calls for attention, a husband and wife need to take time for each other, even when it is inconvenient for either of them to do so. If they can't do so, they need to agree on a time when they can go on a *date* together alone. This is true whether couples are in their first or sixtieth decades of a marriage. Time together can be found on long walks, leaving cell phone or pager at home. When our children were still young enough to need a babysitter for us to go out "on a date together" but old enough to complain about it, we used to tell them, "Mommy and Daddy need this time together." We hoped if it didn't ease their complaint, that it would at least serve as a model someday for their own marriages. It has! Day trips or weekends alone together become crucially important for the husband and wife relationship for the present benefit as well as for the payoff later in life. Such free time together may include having fun and doing things they do not otherwise have time to do, but more important, these are times to talk to each other about the things they choose not to talk about under the pressure of other demands. Talking to each other about aging parents, emerging teenage children, or wonderful grandchildren may carry part of the conversations, but couples need to talk about their own relationship.

It might simply be good to ask each other, "How are we doing?" This is a time to identify the *raw edges* in their relationship. Raw edges are those areas in their relationship where they knowingly or unknowingly periodically *rub each other the wrong way*. They need to talk about ways they communicate better with each other, using that moment of asking as a time to practice the "better" parts. While out on a date or a weekend away from the kids, husband and wife need to say clearly what they need from their relationship for when they return to face the demands of daily living. Talk also needs to include deciding criteria for finding ways to say "No" to others who take away from a husband and wife's time together. Early and mid-years of marriage are critical times for routine, serious conversations

> God meant sensuality and sexual intercourse to be a time of selfless giving of oneself to the other in marriage . . .

between husband and wife.

One of the benefits of having lunch or walks together is that such circumstances force us to be civil to each other and not shout in anger. Silence between tense times on walks together can be constructive as long as couples continue to hold hands as a reminder that they are still connected in their goal of working toward unity. Through these contacts and conversations, when conversations are no longer exclusively arguments, couples have opportunity to discover something greater about themselves and each other than they can think through alone. This is a continuous opportunity to get to know each other more deeply throughout the years of marriage. A husband can now turn his attention back to his wife and a wife can now entrust her attention to her husband once again. In these times, couples need to cultivate a winsome attitude of "us against them" whether "them" is children or work or whatever else causes division, so they can remain undivided in attention and devotion to their marriage.

In Laughter and in Tears

Sexual intercourse can be a time of laughter and a time of tears, both of which can be a good gift of God. Times of laughter can be an expression of complete abandonment to the love and joy that is present in a marriage when all is going well in life. Times of sorrow and grief released in tears can be a time of complete abandonment to the love and comfort that is present in a marriage when all is not going well in life. Such need for the sensual can appear at seemingly strange times in a marriage.

God meant sensuality and sexual intercourse to be a time of selfless giving of oneself to the other in marriage, so it follows that the gift of sensuality that God gives to a marriage can be expressed at different times in different ways. In both youthful newlyweds and in those facing the trials of old age, *making love* is a way to comfort and delight in each other. At playful times and at stressful times the sensual can reassure us that we travel through all things in life together. Being sensually playful in good times and being sensitive to his wife's needs in times of sorrow is part of a husband's calling to take the *lead* by sacrificing his own need for that of his wife's. A wife's flexibility in different times of her husband's needs arises out of her willing submission to *follow* her husband in complete love and trust.

The loss of a job or the experience of an empty house after the children have left home can draw a couple together in mutual comfort in finding each other again. Painful moments in life can surprisingly motivate us to respond sensually. At the death of a parent, for example, a couple may turn to each other for a closeness that can only find fulfillment in the most intimate experience of *making love.* If their life together as husband and wife has been wholesomely sensual all along, it is only natural to bring one's tears as well as laughter to each other in every time of need. Those married couples who share a wholesome sensuality also share a wholesome friendship.

Best Friends

When God created Adam, God declared:

It is not good that the man should be alone; I will make him a helper fit for him. . . . So the LORD God caused a deep sleep to fall upon the man, and while he slept took one of his ribs and closed up its space with flesh. And the rib that the LORD God had taken from the man he made into a woman and brought her to the man. Then the man said, "This at last is bone of my bones and flesh of my flesh; she shall be called Woman, because she was taken out of man." Therefore a man shall leave his father and his mother and hold fast to his wife, and they shall become one flesh. (Genesis 2:18, 21–25)

A husband and wife are many things to each other in marriage, but the first reason God gives for creating a wife for Adam is companionship or friendship—"It is not good that the man should be alone" (Genesis 2:18). So God gave Adam a best friend, his wife, Eve. We could generalize from this and say that it is not good for anyone to be alone in life, for God made each of us for community with Himself and with one another. From this need for others we make acquaintances and neighbors, friends and best friends. From the beginning God intended that husband and wife should become best friends. A best friend is one with whom we can share our deepest dreams and hopes, fears and delights, weaknesses and strengths, and not be rejected for it. Being a best friend in marriage is different than having a best friend outside of marriage. Earlier in this chapter, I recalled a young woman who became a best friend to me and taught me how to dance. In that friendship we both anticipated that that friendship might lead to romance, but it never happened and neither of us was disappointed. Our friendship remained a friendship and she became like a sister to me.

In his book *Aging Well* George Vaillant observes: "A good marriage at age fifty predicted positive aging at eighty."[4] He also reports a wife's interpretation of her relationship to her 70-year-old husband saying, "My

God intended that husband and wife should become best friends.

husband is my best friend; I like looking after him. We have grown closer and fonder every year."[5] Becoming best friends in marriage is the result of taking time for meaningful conversation with each other all along the way of marriage; for a husband it means to "hold fast to his wife" (Genesis 2:24). Becoming best friends increases the potential for sensuality between them even as sexual intercourse may no longer be possible due to disability or illness. A maturing sensuality may simply become a physical "holding fast" to each other in times of weakness and loss. It is enough at times to physically "hold fast" to each other without sexual intercourse, just being content with the comfortable silence that is possible between best friends in marriage. Best friends in marriage know mature love can be expressed sensually in each other's touch and glance as well as in sexual intercourse.

••

4. George Vaillant, *Aging Well*, (New York: Little, Brown, and Company, 2004), 13.
5. Valliant, *Aging Well*, 194.

It is the grace of God and the forgiveness of sins that make us one with each other . . .

Conclusion

This chapter has been about sensuality in marriage. At the same time, it is about relationship. Sensuality without a good relationship between husband and wife is little more than "having sex," which is not enough to enable a marriage to flourish. Being best friends over a lifetime together is much of what contributes to the best of marriages. Most of all, it is the grace of God and the forgiveness of sins that make us one with each other and enables us to "hold fast" to each other while we are both being held by God. My two best friends referred to in the opening pages of this chapter eventually married each other. In my mind, they are still my best friends, even though we seldom have had contact with one another in recent years, but my best friend among best friends is my dance partner, my wife.

two dancing

Two Dancing As One

In order for a couple to ballroom dance beautifully together, they must master the *connections* between them. My wife and I once spent nearly an entire dance lesson just learning how to connect with each other, that is, setting up the frame in preparation for dancing the waltz. Preparation for connecting begins with the man positioning himself properly in order to invite the woman to dance. It continues with the woman accepting the invitation by approaching the man. It happens as follows:

as one

- **Connection 1:** As the man extends his left hand forward shoulder level, inviting the woman to come and accept, the woman steps forward and takes his left hand in her right.
- **Connection 2:** As she steps up to face him, she lines up slightly off center to his right, her waist lightly touching his.
- **Connection 3:** He then places his closed-fingered hand on her back, slightly beneath her left shoulder.
- **Connection 4:** She then places her left hand on his upper arm.

From these connections they end up with the upper body parallel shoulders to shoulders. The man's head is turned slightly to his left as if looking over his wrist, while the woman's head is turned slightly to her left looking over her wrist. This position enables them to keep their balance as they turn and dance. It also enables the man to lead and the woman to sense his lead through the four connections. If they get this right, the real challenge is now to dance through the patterns of the waltz without losing the frame or these connections. It is hard and it is fun and sometimes my wife and I get it just right, but when we don't, the dance falls apart, my leadership fails, and she also falters. As tedious and as difficult as it may be at first to stay connected in this way, it must happen if we want to dance beautifully together. The beauty of a waltz *well-connected* is expressed in its grace and elegance, and in its delight in each other as the two dance as one.

As important as it is for maintaining the connections in dance, it is even more important to maintain the connections in marriage. If a man and woman want to work toward having delight in each other as husband and wife, and if they share a faith in Christ that enables them to experience oneness with God, they must practice the connections that also maintain the oneness between them under God. It begins with the promise of God and their affirmation of the truth:

As is the *connection* between Christ and the Church, so is the *connection* between husband and wife.

> "You are the body of Christ and individually members of it." (1 Corinthians 12:27)

As a Christian I am individually one with God through my faith in Jesus Christ, but at the same time I am also one with all others who are connected by this same faith, including my wife. Individually and together we need to remember and practice the connections with God through public worship where the body of Christ is gathered and in personal devotions where our own connection with Christ is daily fortified. This is true for all Christians but uniquely beneficial in marriage. As is the *connection* between Christ and the Church, so is the *connection* between husband and wife. (See Ephesians 5:31–32.) In addition to the one flesh union called marriage that is shared by all married couples, Christ also invites husband and wife to share in the spiritual connections of the "body of Christ and individually members of it" by means of public worship and in private devotions.

In the liturgy of public worship, where the Word of God is aimed ultimately at proclamation of the Gospel of Christ in our lives, and where the body and blood of Jesus Christ is given to sustain our connections with God and each other, God prepares us for living each day of our marriage. Without these gifts from God given to us, *the body of Christ and individually members of it*, we would falter in life. Without God's gifts given us in the liturgy and in the preaching of public worship, we tend to invent our own ideas of God. We idealize a god in our own mind and make of our god whatever we like him or it to be rather than what the true God really is. Without God's gifts in public worship, in Baptism, absolution, and Holy Communion, we create a god of our own liking who expects nothing of us, is tolerant of everything we do, and blends in with every culturally religious idea that pleases us.

Therefore, if husband and wife neglect the time and place where God comes to them in this uniqueness of public worship, they will also begin to experience the weakening of the connections between them as husband and wife. They may remain married, but their marriage will not flourish as is possible with Jesus Christ. Without public worship they will *individualize* their relationship with God and therefore *individualize* their participation in the marriage, thinking more of *me* than of *us*. This happens when wrongs against each other are not confessed and when forgiveness is not present. In order to make their marriage a most beautiful dance throughout life, they must worship God together and recognize that they are part of *the body of Christ and individually members of it*.

PRACTICING DANCING

There are times when I need to practice alone a dance step or a styling technique in which I will eventually lead my wife when we dance together. I find that it is important that each of us learn our own parts separately rather than together, for when we practice together, it becomes clear that my wife and I learn at different rates of speed and have difficulties that each must resolve if we are to dance well together. I discovered early in our dancing that if we only practice as a couple, this interferes with my learning to lead because my wife tends to anticipate rather than to follow my lead, resulting in us moving in two different directions. This leads to disaster on the dance floor and requires a quick recovery if we are to continue.

There is another problem in only practicing as a couple. When we practice as a couple, we are distracted by each other's mistakes. It is therefore necessary that we practice dancing alone at times to focus on our own part in the dance first. Although our goal is to dance together, I, as the one responsible for leading, have to know the patterns of a dance and how to take the lead in them before I can expect my wife to follow.

Something similar is true of our spiritual life together as a couple. Together, we attend public worship—I would miss sitting next to my wife if she were not there—but I also find that there are times when I need to be alone with God. I need

> Though difficult, it is necessary for husbands and wives to be intentional about setting time aside for prayer and meditative Bible reading.

a regular time and place for personal devotions and so does she. *Personal devotions* in the morning are a good way to start the day when, without the distraction of others around us, we are able to read the Word of God, think about it, and pray about our concerns for the day ahead. This means more than a brief prayer while driving to the grocery store or on the way to work, though these times are opportune substitutes occasionally.

Though difficult, it is necessary for husbands and wives to be intentional about setting time aside for prayer and meditative Bible reading. This is no easy task for a mother of young children, or for both husband and wife who work eight or more hours outside the home. While at home they may rightly believe it is important to spend what remaining time there is with the children. It may be that some times in life are easier than others for sustaining a personal devotional life, but it is also true that personal devotions are most needed when our lives are too busy to sustain them. The important thing is to begin, come back to, and work at personal devotions throughout our lives.

Most people who are conscientious about this find that they falter in sustaining regular daily devotions because of unexpected crises, on-going exhaustion, or endless interruptions. This is normal, and neither guilt nor weariness ought to discourage us from returning to the practice. Although I am unwilling to recommend this to anyone else, I find that I maintain the *connection* better when I do so four or five days out of the week, allowing a Friday and/or a Saturday to pass without morning devotions. Sunday morning puts me back in the habit by means of public worship, and I return in earnest to personal devotions again Monday through Thursday. I suppose this planned benign neglect works for me because my desire for personal devotions is renewed by its occasional planned absence.

Although my wife and I always pray together in bed before falling asleep at night, we are usually too tired to take on the resolving of things on our minds, so we use this brief time of prayer together to put things in God's hands until we can deal with them in the morning. We have learned through experience that late night disagreements bring out the worst in us and, unless they interfere with a good night's sleep, we avoid them. In the morning, before discussing them, we each have our own personal devotions. Consequently, I rise in the morning and go to my study where I can close the door and be alone to practice my connection with God. My wife does the same in her quiet area of the house.

We have each practiced morning devotional time most of our married life. In my daily personal devotions I can *practice* my part in keeping the *connections* with my wife by praying for her encouragement in things I know she must face that day. Or, when we have had a disagreement, I can practice confessing my wrong and receive forgiveness before God so that I may do and receive the same before my wife. I may find that there is something my wife does that has angered me, and I need to pray for wisdom to know how and when to discuss it with her. When we have been busy and have had little time for each other, I can rehearse the importance of our time together, calling on God to help me to be willing to make time for her. As in leading in dance, I can also practice my leadership in our life together, asking for God's guidance in doing so in wisdom and love. Personal devotions with my wife in mind is a way of practicing the *connections* between us as she does the same with me in mind.

It requires a conscious decision to practice personal devotions daily, and encouragement from each other to continue. If one falters in his or her spiritual connections by neglecting a personal devotional life, there needs to be a mutually agreeable arrangement to call attention to the effect this has on each of them and on their marriage as a one flesh union. Calling each other to account in this is not to be done by accusation, complaint, or blaming, but by encouragement, patience, and the periodic gentle reminder that the faltering partner needs to return to his or her spiritual connections for the benefit of both of them. If this is agreed upon ahead of time, it will not be perceived as nagging and they can think of winsome ways to do this together. Those who share a spiritual life know the weakness of human nature and so they bear one another's burdens in encouraging each other to continue in public worship and in personal devotions.

There are devotional booklets to assist us in this discipline of personal devotional life, but what we need more than anything is *time* that allows us to think and pray. In reading a portion of the Bible we need to have time to think about its meaning for us. In taking time to pray we might begin with a psalm or the Lord's Prayer as we pray in public worship to keep our prayers connected to the body of Christ as well as our own needs. Our personal devotions should be shaped by our public worship, for personal devotions grow out of the public body of Christ at worship.

Practicing the Connections Together

My wife and I do not practice dance just for the sake of practice, but after practicing we find that dancing socially is a lot more gratifying. Whether or not we dance well together depends on how well we have practiced and know our part. Every few months, my wife and I find that we have worked long and hard on a new dance step only to have neglected an old one that now needs relearning. It is disheartening that our hard work in the past was not enough, but we were encouraged by the discovery that even our instructors need daily practice to maintain their skills. Moreover, we soon discovered that sometimes the reason we had forgotten the original steps of a dance is that we had improved and moved on to a more advanced way of doing the steps. Progress in learning to dance, as in most things, seems to be three steps forward and two back.

Growth in learning to appreciate and practice being one flesh as husband or wife also sometimes seems to be an experience of three steps forward and two back. As it is difficult, complicated, and demanding in learning to dance, so it can be in marriage. One of the most difficult things to do is to speak openly and freely to each other about personal spiritual struggles. Sometimes, after my wife and I have spent time alone in prayer, we come together to pray. The time before we come together has put us in touch with ourselves and with God in a way that carries over into our time together. When we come together, we first read a text from the Bible, and then talk about it in its personal meaning for each of our lives. This is not so much a time for Bible study as it is a

> Times together that allow for self-disclosure are built on the foundations of trust constructed between husband and wife over the years.

devotional look at us in our relationship with God and each other. As we talk, our thoughts, fears, concerns, anxieties, and problems surface. Having established a trust between us over the years, this time of self-exposure is routine, even though it is sometimes painful to face things in ourselves we have not faced up to that point or that continue to reappear with little hope of solution.

Times together that allow for self-disclosure are built on the foundations of trust constructed between husband and wife over the years. In speaking openly to each other we discover things about each other and ourselves that we did not recognize before. These discoveries provide a challenge for further growth in us personally as well as in our relationship. The benefit of this devotional time together is that we can support each other in confession and forgiveness when needed as well as in loving and caring for each other when one or both of us is hurting. As we finally conclude our devotional time by putting our conversation into prayer together, we bare our souls to God and to each other and find healing and renewed strength in our relationship with God and with each other. All of this takes time. We often spend a good hour together after our time apart in devotions. This is not possible to do every day, but we do so when we feel the need, and it paves the way for better connections between us in our marriage and in our relationship with God.

Maintaining the Spiritual Connections

My wife and I find that we devote more time to practicing dancing in the summer than we do in the winter. Nevertheless, each fall we press on and work at making time for dancing, just as after being newlyweds we had to work at making time for our practicing the spiritual connections in our marriage. The dawn of a new life together after our wedding settled into the routine of daily life. As the years passed by, our marriage continued to make good progress, but we had to discipline ourselves to protect what we had become together and plan for what we hoped to become together in the future. Our friends were facing infidelity and divorce and we did not want to neglect practicing the connections in our marriage and end up down that road. Moreover, there were changes taking place in the world around us competing for our marriage.

In the dawning of the age in which our generation became young adults, the availability of the birth control pill threatened to weaken the link between sex and marriage. Premarital sex became virtually risk free with the lessened chance of pregnancy, and the need for marriage was conveniently avoided. The legalization of abortion further eroded the connection between sex, pregnancy, and marriage. What you permit, you also encourage. The abortion industry flourished as women's rights groups began to call for the right to end the life of the child within.

Feeding the freedom frenzy, feminists encouraged women to be free of all social and moral inhibition, urging women to find fulfillment outside the bond (or bondage) of marriage and family. A greater number of women made the choice between career and an existing marriage, choosing to seek fulfillment in career rather than in marriage and family. The value of marriage was traded for the value of greater freedom. Divorce gained greater social acceptance. The bonding of divorced women was encouraged and became available through support systems once provided by marriage and family at home. Women bonded for support in everything from collegiality with breast cancer survivors, to exercise and diet programs, to classes in exotic techniques of meditation. Staying attentive to marriage and family for both husband and wife in a world that offers an increasing opportunity for bonding outside of marriage and family requires a willpower that few seemingly managed to maintain.

Even these families are challenged and threatened by over-active lifestyles that leave increasingly less time for each family. This problem was portrayed in the movie *Shall We Dance?* (2004), where the husband was unwilling to call into question the family's busy lifestyle and instead began taking dance lessons without his wife, even as she pressed on with her own career and circle of support. It was not that these family members did not care deeply for one another, but rather that they simply didn't have time for one another. The result of this husband's reluctance to take the lead in his marriage and family and call attention to their lifestyles led to his wife's suspicion that he was having an affair after work. Even when she found out that he was not unfaithful, she still felt left out of his life and the distance between them increased.

Shall We Dance? shows that as the summer of our lives passes us by, the winter months of life assault us with a lifestyle of monotonous routine activity that looked promising when we began,

> Spiritual connection begins with Christ's love for us.

but lost luster with the passage of time. The connections between husband and wife begin to crumble under the meaninglessness of hyperactive, stress-filled lives. As in dancing, it is hard to go back to the ease of practicing in summer when you are trapped in the deadening grip of winter. Something has to happen to free us from the temptation to look for fulfillment in more and more activity. Husbands and wives have to practice the spiritual connections that bring them together in Christ. Spiritual connection begins with Christ's love for us.

In *Life Together*, Dietrich Bonhoeffer observes that human love differs from spiritual love: "Human love is directed to the other person for his own sake, spiritual love loves him for Christ's sake."[1] Human love between husband and wife is fed by what we like about and benefit from in each other and lasts as long as *likes* and *benefits* continue. Human love can last a lifetime, even growing deeper as likes and benefits increase, but it can also grow cold and die when husband and wife find other *likes* and *benefits* elsewhere. Human love alone can never know the spiritual love for each other that is found in Christ's love for us and our love for Him. Spiritual love for a spouse, on the other hand, is a gift from God to us received by faith as husband and wife continue to maintain the connections with God.

••

1.   Dietrich Bonhoeffer, *Life Together* (New York: Harper, 1954), 34.

Practicing the spiritual connections of public worship and personal devotions keeps spiritual love alive in us. In Christ's love, not only are we loved, but our love for husband or wife also becomes the deepest kind of love a marriage can experience. We find that we have begun to love spouse not only for who he or she is as a person, but also because we love Christ alive in that spouse. The bond of love is eternal, continuing forever not as human love, but as spiritual love that comes to us in even richer measure with the newness of the day of Resurrection. There may be times when a husband or wife may not be the recipient of the *likes and benefit* of human love because serious illness, burdensome anxiety, or crushing self-doubt interfere, but Christ's love in us loves beyond the likes and benefits received in marriage. The spiritual connections in public worship and personal devotions together and alone rebuild human love and seriously surpass it with spiritual love as we grow in faith and love for Christ.

WHEN YOU GO TO THE DANCE ALONE

Each time my wife and I attend a social dance I notice that there are always more women than men on the sideline waiting for someone with whom to dance. Occasionally, with my wife's blessing, I may ask another woman to dance because I know how much I enjoy dancing and would hate for her to miss out on it. It is interesting that more women than men come to a dance alone, just as more women than men attend public worship on a Sunday morning. The plurality of women in either case may be attributed to several possibilities: women live longer than men and there are more of them; younger women tend to come to public worship even without their husbands for the benefit of their children; women generally seem to sense the need for the spiritual life more naturally than men.

My mother was the first to attend church in our family. She began attending public worship because a local pastor knocked on her door shortly after we moved to town and invited her. I was soon enrolled in Sunday School and I attended public worship regularly with my mother. My father and mother had a good marriage, but Dad joined us in church attendance only later when I was 16 years old. Eventually, Dad joined the church and we became a family in maintaining the connections with God and with one another. It is difficult when a wife pays attention to her spiritual connection with Christ and her husband does not. My mother's gentle patience and love for my father bore similarities to St. Augustine's mother, Monica, in the fourth century. Augustine's father was not a Christian. Unlike other wives who gathered at the river to do laundry and complain about their husbands, Monica did not complain, but prayed for her husband. When her husband was eventually baptized, his old life became a new life, and the spiritual connections between them blossomed.

THE UNBELIEVING SPOUSE

It is not easy when one marriage partner has faith in Christ and the other does not. This means that the unbelieving spouse cannot return the spiritual love that the unbelieving spouse receives from the believer. It is still lonely when human love is mutually genuine, but spiritual love is not returned. Even more painful is the experience of a Christian whose unbelieving spouse is able to sustain neither human love nor spiritual love. Paul comments on wives or husbands who are married to unbelievers. He was asked whether the believing spouse should agree to a divorce if the unbelieving spouse asks for one. Paul writes rhetorically, "Wife, how do you know whether you will save your husband? Husband, how do you know whether your will save your wife?" (1 Corinthians 7:16). You don't know! Paul's advice is therefore to let the unbelieving partner go, even though God intends marriage to be indissoluble.

In the New Testament, marriage between a Christian spouse and an unbelieving spouse raises the question, "Should I as a Christian be married to an unbelieving spouse? And, if I am married to one, will it jeopardize my relationship with God?" Paul reassured the believing spouse that God would sanctify (make holy) their relationship. God says through Paul, "The unbelieving husband is made holy because of his wife, and the unbelieving wife is made holy because of her husband" (1 Corinthians 7:14). But we must understand the meaning of the word *holy* as it is used here. In the book of Leviticus, addressed to the Old Testament people of God, God spoke to the issue of His people's need to be made holy; "You shall be holy, for I the LORD Your God am holy" (Leviticus 19:2). This is important because no one is acceptable to God unless he is willing to be a made a participant in God's holiness. Holiness is not something we can produce through our behavior but something God shares with us if we are willing to receive it as a gift in the forgiveness of sins. God alone is holy and His holy nature stands in opposition to human beings because all human nature is contaminated by sin. Sin and holiness are opposed to each other but God cleanses from sin and shares His holiness with His people. God showed the Old Testament people how they could be made holy through the forgiveness of sins when they offered a bull, a sheep, or a goat to the priest as a sacrifice for their sins.

In the New Testament Jesus Christ became our sacrifice for sin through His death on the cross, ending the need for all further sacrifices. Those who put their trust in Jesus Christ share in God's holiness. In answer to the question raised at the beginning of this discussion, God says He will

. . . it is vital that the believing spouse participate in public worship and personal devotions to the benefit of the unbelieving spouse, praying always for that spouse and their marriage.

consider the unbelieving husband as holy for the believing wife's sake and not allow the unbeliever's participation in the marriage to contaminate the holiness of the believing spouse. Likewise, God will consider their children as holy for otherwise they "would be unclean [contaminated]" (1 Corinthians 7:14). Holiness, however, extended by God to the unbelieving spouse does not imply salvation for that spouse—salvation comes only by grace through faith in Jesus Christ. (See Romans 3:23.) Yet the unbelieving spouse lives in the presence of God through the believing spouse's participation in the marriage.

Whatever distress an unbelieving spouse may be to a believing spouse, the believing spouse must remember that if God is willing to treat an unbelieving spouse as if he or she were holy, then the believing spouse had better not discount the unbelieving spouse but love that spouse humanly and spiritually all the more. To keep up the connection it is vital that the believing spouse participate in public worship and personal devotions to the benefit of the unbelieving spouse, praying always for that spouse and their marriage. It may be that the unbelieving spouse will come to faith in Jesus Christ.[2]

Conclusion

In a good marriage husband and wife grow throughout the length of it. There may setbacks that stall growth for a while, but as they work through the dry and difficult times they rediscover each other in new and satisfying ways. They become sensitive to each other's needs and their affection for each other reflects it. Expressed sensually, this means that they move from merely being guided by their feelings for each other to being guided by the meaningfulness of the relationship itself. Whether they continue to make love or simply find comfort in each other's arms, their sensuality can continue to mature. In the end, when the years are added up, the best of marriages produce the best of friends. It is a gift of God that the two have remained one and learned to delight in it together.

2. "Likewise, wives, be subject to your own husbands, so that even if some do not obey the word, they may be won without a word by the conduct of their wives—when they see your respectful and pure conduct" (1 Peter 3:1–2).

maintaining

Maintaining the Frame

In ballroom dance the importance of *maintaining the frame* is impressed on a student during each dance lesson. The frame consists in maintaining a good posture in which the arms of both man and woman are held up firmly and in place with all the *connections* between them as described in chapter 5. This frame is what enables the couple to move as one, with each knowing where they are headed as a couple. A good frame is necessary for the woman to separate from the man in order to make a three hundred and sixty degree turn, then return to him.

the frame

. . . a good marriage is also something to be taken with you out into the world.

Maintaining an upright posture enables the couple to keep balance in relationship to each other. If even a part of the frame, either arms or posture, begins to misalign, the feet will not follow and the dance pattern will suffer. Just as maintaining the frame in dance allows a smooth separation and return of the partner, so the same in marriage enables each spouse to separate, interact appropriately with others outside the marriage, and return home again to each other's waiting arms.

The truth is that it is hard to separate a good marriage from the outside world. A good marriage is pleasant to come home to at the end of the day, but a good marriage is also something to be taken with you out into the world. A good marriage is not a dance trophy to be stored and adored on a shelf, but a gift to be shared! For the husband or wife whose relationship with Christ calls for sharing the faith and its benefits, a good marriage taken along into the world is a vocation of its own. A husband benefits by having his wife as the companion with whom he can share his greatest dreams and his worst fears, knowing that she will support him at home and out in the world. A wife benefits by having a husband whose love provides the security she needs to cope with life at home with the children and in the work place and out in the community.

There is no place like home where a good marriage is rich with satisfaction, where a husband and wife have learned to know, understand, and accept each other after years of practice in making the marriage work for them. Satisfaction does not require a perfect marriage, but it does require mutual human love and is enriched more so by spiritual love on the part of one spouse or both. Building a good marriage, where the basic requirement of human love is present, is like building a good frame in dance that allows movement as one. Building a good marriage where both human love and spiritual love are present adds the delight that is present in both marriage and dance.

Marriage fulfills the need for intimate companionship and promotes confidence because of security, so a husband and wife will be able to reach out beyond themselves to others. They can move back and forth between the world and their marriage freely, maintaining the balance between meeting their own needs and contributing to the needs of others. Maintaining the frame enables a husband and wife to leave the comfort of marriage *for a time* in order to interact with others.

Because a good marriage is something we carry within us, we never really leave it behind, but move into the lives of others because our needs have been met in our marriage. We will find people whose need for intimacy and companionship is not met through marriage, either because they are single, divorced, have lost a spouse through death, or have a spouse with mental or medical limitations. Our willingness to include them in the community of our friendship is a vocation for those of us whose needs are met in our marriage, remembering that meeting the needs of others is always to be balanced by attention to our own needs as a couple as well. Meeting the needs of others may be as simple as speaking to someone on the phone once or twice a week or as complex as sharing our home when they need a place to come to for support. Couples need to be aware that not all people's needs can be appropriately met by inviting them into our homes. Some people are more needy than even a healthy marriage environment can help and should be referred to counseling for those needs.

LIVING FAITHFULLY IN THE WORLD

It is easier to attend Friday night practice at the dance studio than it is to move beyond this environment to attend public dances in the community. The dances at the studio are among supportive teachers and fellow-students. The dances in the community are among many who have little connection with one another and become competitors for floor space and attention. On a crowded public dance floor there is more stepping on toes, literally and figuratively. This will always happen when crowds are filled with strangers dancing with enthusiasm. When dancers accidentally do interfere with one another, most people apologize immediately and maintain a sense of humor, but occasionally there is a couple or two who have little regard for others and who dominate the dance floor to the detriment of others. Dancing among people with whom there is little relationship is always a challenge that calls for skillfulness and forgiveness. As in ballroom dancing, moving back and forth from the comfortable and supportive to the challenging and the uncomfortable is a pattern required of most of us throughout life.

BECAUSE OUR NEEDS ARE MET

A good marriage is a comfortable place to live, but life requires that a husband and wife also live in the sometimes uncomfortable world beyond the comfort of their marriage. The sometimes uncomfortable is experienced in the daily interaction with those whose marriages are failing, those who have contempt for marriage and live promiscuously, and those whose infidelity is paraded brazenly. The comfort of a good marriage that counters this experience is built on a rich intimacy and a satisfying security. The *intimacy* in a good marriage is both physical and relational, as chapter 4 illustrates. The *security* in a good marriage is based on knowing who and whose you are as husband and wife, in Christ.

Living in the intimacy and security of a good marriage gives a couple freedom and support to interact with others in the world. Immaturity, mental health problems, excessive stress, hardships, physical distance from each other over time, and many other things can cause the ties of intimacy and security in a marriage to weaken. When this begins to happen, the temptation to idealize relationships with strangers and to participate in adulterous relationships can destroy whatever intimacy and security is left in a marriage. It may begin with a husband (or wife) mentally comparing his spouse with someone he works with, fantasizing that what is not being met in his relationship with his wife could be met in a relationship with this person. Infidelity is a temptation that attacks the heart of a marriage. Lack of fulfillment in a marriage never justifies infidelity but calls for both spouses to remain faithful to God and to each other as they work at the renewal of their

Infidelity is not the *cause* of marriage problems, but the *result* of something gone wrong in the marriage.

marriage with the help of a counselor.

Infidelity is not the *cause* of marriage problems but the *result* of something gone wrong in the marriage. Infidelity need not be expressed in the traditional form of adultery, but may also be expressed in devotion to something other than one's marriage. In the movie *Shall We Dance?* John's wife hired a detective to follow him, anticipating that he might be having an affair with another woman. When his wife found out that he was not having an affair, but was taking dancing lessons without her, she still felt betrayed. As a marriage breaks down, a husband and wife who do not recognize what is happening will find fidelity shifts to other things and other people. A wife may shift her fidelity to her children in devoting her life to them to the neglect of her husband. A husband may shift his fidelity to his work, finding more reasons to spend more time away from his wife for the sake of his work. When fidelity shifts, the marriage is in trouble and needs attention immediately, no matter how long it has been going on.

As I did pastoral counseling with women unhappy in their marriages, there were a few who tried to shift their fidelity to me as someone whom they felt cared about them and listened sympathetically to their complaints. It is easy to idealize a counselor because he provides everything needed for intimacy and security in the counseling relationship. Because my need for intimacy and security were fulfilled elsewhere, in the love between my wife and me, it was not a problem for me to deal with these women, but it was difficult for these women who were hungry for a relationship. Because I did not signal a reciprocal need as they might have anticipated, they could experience my counsel as objective as they worked through their need for a relationship with their own spouse. As one divorced woman struggled with this painful experience in her life, she referred to my marriage several times as "good." I asked her if my "good" marriage was a discouragement to her after all she had been through in several unsuccessful marriages. She replied eagerly that, much to the contrary, my marriage gave her hope that marriage such as my wife and I shared was in fact possible, something she had not been sure of in recent years.

Although infidelity most often leads to divorce, it need not. The wounds of infidelity are extremely deep and painful, sometimes causing one or the other to question whether he or she will ever be capable of sustaining a meaningful relationship in marriage. There are some couples that overcome infidelity that has led to adultery. For those rare couples willing to be honest with themselves and with each other, and who seek counseling, there may be opportunity to rebuild a marriage relationship from the ground up. It first requires a willingness to do so. In the end, forgiveness for infidelity is essential. Forgiveness requires (1) honest self-examination, (2) recognition of that which each person contributed to the resulting infidelity, (3) recognition of the needs of each in the marriage, and (4) the willingness to let go of the anger between them that prevents them from forgiving each other. It is as difficult to work at reconciliation as it is to work through a divorce, but the end result is gratifying in the former and full of lingering grief in the latter.

To remain faithful in marriage we have to *dance* out in the world, not always in each other's presence, but always on each other's mind. This is not to say that a husband or wife must be

We ought to be aware of temptation, but not threatened by its presence. conscious of the other at every moment, but it does mean each will be shaped by the image of the other when a situation arises in which to be distracted from one's spouse would be harmful. A man on a business trip interacting with a businesswoman over lunch needs to maintain a social distance that gives a clear message of fidelity to his wife. A woman in a committee meeting with men needs to be aware of the inappropriate attention paid to her that seems more than is called for. People are attracted to each other for many reasons, and naiveté is a dangerous companion. We ought to be aware of temptation, but not threatened by its presence. And we ought to be mindful of our spouse that surpasses the immediate temptation.

The question that is often raised is whether a married woman can be a friend to a married man without it having implications for intimacy. The answer is in the negative because nearly all human beings require intimacy somewhere in life. The important thing is to recognize temptation when it is present, to consciously admit it, and to let it go as quickly as possible, not toying with it in fantasy. A man, recognizing that he finds a woman other than his wife to be attractive, is being honest with himself. The same is true for a wife toward a man other than her husband. Attraction is the capacity required for finding a person desirable that made it possible for each of us to find each other as husband and wife in the beginning. That capacity is always a part of us, but couples committed to and secure in their love for each other can appreciate the attractiveness of others without indulging in infidelity either briefly considered or acted upon.

Attraction itself is not enough to justify either infidelity within marriage or promiscuity outside marriage. Many people live together with full physical intimacy outside of marriage, simulating intimacy to test what marriage might be like. It is as if they are sticking one toe in the water to see how warm or cold it feels. Those who are unmarried may base their whole prospect of marriage on this test of feelings, waiting to feel right before committing to marriage. It is naive to believe that feelings or experience alone can tell us what is required to make a marriage work. Those who have lived together outside of marriage and consequently become newlyweds quickly learn that feelings change daily as each discovers the real person behind the mask worn while living together before marriage. It is not surprising that the rate of divorce is higher among those who have lived together before marriage than it is for those who did not.

It is necessary for a couple to set limits to their passion before it becomes a problem, and then to set up behaviors, situations, and interventions to prevent their passion from taking control of their lives too quickly. Passion needs to be limited by talking to each other about it. Before marriage my wife and I talked continuously, revealing our deeper selves to each other. We talked about our goals in life and our desire to build a marriage and family together around our common faith in Christ. Those who have built on the solid ground of maintaining the frame and all its connections know that it is by the grace of God and not by human willpower alone that a marriage works well. Love covers a multitude of sins, but love does not justify the sin of infidelity, adultery, or premarital immorality. A sexual morality based on feelings misunderstood as love, and which lacks the faithfulness toward God's intent for marriage, misleads all who hope for more in life than they receive.

TIME FOR EACH OTHER

I must admit that as a husband bearing responsibility for the lead in maintaining balance in our marriage, I jealously guard the time my wife and I need together in order to keep our marriage on solid ground. I am jealous, not of other people, but of our time together in the sense that God is a jealous God who requires that His relationship with us be our highest priority. There are times when both my wife and I decline an invitation simply in order to have time with each other, such as on a Friday evening when we can dance or go out to dinner or just watch a movie at home. Marriage requires this so that the priority of being husband and wife never slips into second place to our work or to excessive devotion to other activities or friendships outside the marriage. This does not mean a husband should be possessive or *control* his wife's time with others, but that he bears responsibility for taking the lead in discussing with his wife their need to guard their time together. In many marriages it may be the wife who makes their time together a priority, but a husband ought to take this as a reminder of his own calling to guard their time as well.

Time together does not always take priority over all things. A couple may, by mutual agreement, need to limit their time together where the

. . . it is by the grace of God and not by human willpower alone that a marriage works well.

attention of one or both is needed elsewhere for a while. But a marriage and those within it must never be completely sacrificed for it. When my wife's physical health began to suffer as a result of doing the major part of caring for my aging mother, I moved my mother to a good care facility permanently in order for my wife to recover her health. We both continued to support my mother at her new home, but it relieved my mother of guilt for requiring so much of us and it enabled us to attend to others as well as ourselves. A husband ought to take the lead in *maintaining the frame*, balancing the needs of others and the needs of the marriage, and if he does not, his wife ought to gently remind him of his calling to do so.

Married couples need to learn how to set limits on their invitation to others to call or "drop in any time." My wife once became a friend to an elderly woman who had never married and who had lived independently until she became ill and moved into an assisted living facility temporarily. At first my wife willingly offered to do chores in her apartment for her, to take her to the doctor when necessary, and generally offer support, but the requests for time and attention increased and my wife had to suggest that this woman make a list of things needed so that when my wife visited her one day each week they could go over the list together. Between visits, they came to an agreement that their phone conversations would be limited to once or twice a week for encouragement and support. Of course, emergency needs are always fair ground for breaking the rules.

Setting limits works to the benefit of both. As we reach out to share the benefits of our own gifts received in marriage, we also have to set limits for ourselves and others in order to maintain the frame of marriage. Limits protect our time and call for an anxious person to exercise self-discipline. Setting limits allows us to support persons God has placed in our path for His care. The lonely, the troubled, the grieving, and those who have no one with whom to share their thoughts and fears can be beneficiaries of the grace of God through us whose needs are met in our marriage. There is a vocation as husband and wife among those whose needs are left unmet in this world in which we can be a friend or support in time of need. If our own needs for intimacy and companionship are foundationally met at home in our marriage, we will have much to offer.

A Need for Our Own Kind

In a large social gathering husband and wife who come as a couple frequently temporarily separate; women end up talking with women and men among men. As much as men and women need each other, men need to separate themselves from women to be among men and women need to do the same. Each speaks a language understood only entirely by their own kind. In marriage this difference in *language* is overcome by years of effort and generosity of spirit that is bound by the commitment to marriage itself.

For ten years, a group of six to ten men have met at my home once a month for intellectual conversation. We are all university professors of English, theology, history, philosophy, political science, and the humanities in general. I belong to another group of men, accompanied by their wives and a few single women, who meet monthly at various pubs to discuss the common love of the English sports car, the MG. We are engineers, salesmen, auto mechanics, teachers, businessmen, entrepreneurs, and more. In both of these groups—university intellectuals and car buffs—we find common ground because we are men who enjoy the company of men. Likewise, for ten or more years my wife has hosted a weekly quilting group of eight to six women at our home in which support and friendship draws them to come even when no quilting project is forthcoming. Further, my wife periodically fills in for teaching a women's Bible Class at church that brings out women and their toddlers as much for their interaction as for their study together.

Men seldom talk about relationships; we talk about ideas and our cars. We seldom talk about our wives or families unless there is something that calls for support from a fellow husband or father who sympathizes with us in our pain. Between men with men there is talk that women find uncomfortable, not because there is anything immoral or inappropriate about it, but simply because it is "guy talk." Between women there is also a language of their own. Men who come with their wives to large social gatherings often excuse themselves to join the nearest gathering of men where they can be who they are with greater comfort. Men and women who have a good marriage reflect this goodness in the way they talk about and treat the opposite sex in general, even while they are among other men. This doesn't mean that men don't joke about women as women, just as women joke about men as men. There is in part a discomfort between the sexes that is a social reflection of the ambivalence between how close and how distant a man and a woman should be to each other when married to someone else. Therefore, men with men and women with women are drawn to their own kind to sort out the challenges in life, both personal and vocational.

OUR LIVES BEAR WITNESS

Among friends we are drawn to, some might share our faith in Christ and some might not. Before finding a common ground of faith people are usually drawn to each other by virtue of personalities that blend well together. It is often only after a friendship has reached a certain point that it may be discovered that there is a common ground of faith in God or not. It need not be the goal of one who has faith in Christ to only befriend those who share that faith. If *God so loved the world that He gave His only begotten Son* for all, we ought also to give ourselves to others in Christ's name, even if the speaking of that name is not that which draws us together.

We bear witness to our faith in Christ most genuinely by the transformation of our lives and only after that by our words. When others meet Christ in us, it is because of this transformation that others are open to our words about Christ. When the relationship between friends deepens and inquiry is made or need cries out for it, the sharing of our faith in words becomes genuine. This solidarity with people as people is what Christ accomplished in becoming a man so that He could go to the cross for all who would have otherwise been lost without Him. The vocation of a husband and wife with faith in Christ is, if possible, to draw into Christ those whom God places in our path. Our life in Christ to others means bearing the sign of God's love for them through, among other things, the witness of our marriage as a blessing to others.

Part of the witness of our life in Christ is to decline those things that counter our witness. As faith deepens in us, it takes its toll on our inappropriate desires. A husband or wife whose needs are met in marriage have different values than those still on the road to finding fulfillment in this world. Although personalities may always reflect the weaknesses of a sinful human nature even in a Christian, a faithful Christian cannot carelessly indulge his sinful nature and long retain his peace with Christ. Being friends with those who do not share faith in Christ may cause an awkward moment that needs to be addressed. These awkward moments ought not be made more awkward by preaching a moralistic sermon, but must still reflect a genuine friendship even with the one with whom we disagree. The uniqueness of the Christian witness is to love your *enemies* even when your *enemies* are your friends. There is much that is genuine even between friends who do not share a common faith in Christ. We are always to live in the world without being part of the world, and to be a witness to Christ in us and in our marriage.

> We are always to live in the world without being a part of the world, and to be a witness to Christ in us and in our marriage.

CONCLUSION

Dancing with someone other than your spouse can be awkward or may be pleasant, but no two people dance together as well as those who have practiced it together for years. The same is true for marriage. Interaction with others outside the marriage is inevitable and a good marriage can shape us for interacting faithfully. A good marriage can also be a blessing to others who have either remained single or are divorced or have suffered the death of a spouse. We are blessed in marriage to be a blessing to others. If marriage is, as God says, a reflection of the nature of the relationship between Christ and His Church, so a blessing of a good marriage is to share the results of what God has given us with others. The longer a good marriage lasts before death claims one or both partners, the more of a witness it is to those who see it as a sign of hope for their own lives.

the Lord

THE LORD OF THE DANCE
AGING WELL TOGETHER

began this book by noting that my mother and father met on the dance floor in 1934 and danced until my father died at age 94. As a child, I remember that they danced socially most weekends at the American Legion Hall. When they retired to Florida, they danced on Saturday nights at a yacht club. Dancing aged them well; it kept them young, healthy, and vibrant. My mother, twelve years younger than my father, lived to be 95. This is not to say that everyone who dances lives that long, but my parent's fifty-plus years of marriage was surely enhanced by it.

of the dance

"He who finds a wife finds a good thing and obtains favor from the LORD" (Proverbs 18:22).

At Harvard University, in a continuing study of adult development in men that began in 1938, along with a similar study of women at Stanford University, and also of inner city men, the seminal question was asked: "Why do some people age well and others not?"[1] This is not a study of health issues associated with aging, but of why some people age well, particularly in terms of attitude and happiness. An interesting finding in the study concluded: "A good marriage at age fifty predicted positive aging at eighty."[2]

The present director of the study, George Vaillant, continues to follow the same men and women who were part of the original study, noting the factors that led to their aging well. Among the factors, he found that learning to *play* throughout life is important.[3] I would suggest that ballroom dancing is a good example of play between husband and wife. Vaillant also found that being *creative* in dealing with life's roadblocks leads to aging well. Additionally, the study found that making new friends, as old friends are lost, is more important to positive aging than retirement income. According to the study, it is not our struggles that predict aging well as much as it is the good people who come into our lives. Perhaps most important, the study concluded that life is enriched by loving a particular person. In other words, a good marriage predicts positive aging.

••

1. George Vaillant, *Aging Well* (New York: Little, Brown, and Company, 2004), Appendix A.
2. Vaillant, *Aging Well*, 13.
3. Vaillant, *Aging Well*, 224.

In this chapter I will focus on the importance of marriage for positive aging, illustrating what the biblical writer says: "He who finds a wife finds a good thing and obtains favor from the LORD" (Proverbs 18:22).

To say that a good marriage leads to a long life would not be accurate. However, to say that a good marriage contributes to aging well does seem to be accurate, according to reputable studies. In the study cited above, happiness and satisfaction in old age had little to do with accumulation of wealth—it had everything to do with relationships. This is not surprising to Christians, but it is interesting to have it verified in the study. Throughout this book I have tried to express the importance of a good marriage both on the basis of God's promises and from my own experience. By the grace of God, short of salvation itself, my wife is the best thing that has ever happened to me. Any snapshot of a particular day in our marriage may not evidence perfection, but on the whole our marriage has been all that my wife and I could have asked for.

I remember a conversation with a couple in my church office asking me to officiate at their wedding. I felt a twinge of concern as I watched the woman direct her fiancé to sit against a wall at the back of my study, while she pulled her chair up to my desk close enough to touch the desk with her knees. As the conversation unfolded, it turned out that she had already been married four times and this was her fifth attempt at success. I tried gently to explore the reasons for the previous failures and she listed each ex-husband's faults for me in detail. When I asked what her own contribution to the failure of the marriage might have been, she sat up straight, seemingly insulted by my

Lifelong learning is essential to a good marriage.

question. I explained that I was only concerned that she not repeat similar patterns of behaviors that might lead to the failure of this fifth attempt at marriage. When I realized that she could take no responsibility for her part in the failures, it became clear that I could not, in good conscience, contribute to another failure by performing this wedding. Exasperated, she slumped back in her chair and said, "Well, that's what every other clergyman in town has said to me," as if to say, "What's wrong with all of you?"

Both my parents had been married before they married each other. Their first marriages were short-lived and ended in divorce. The fact that their second marriage, of which I was a part, lasted for over fifty years attests to the fact that something changed in how they approached relationships, as is often the case following a divorce. In their second attempt at marriage my parents became best friends, their marriage flourished, and they aged well. The change in my parent's success at marriage was not just that of a new partner, but a change in each of them and the determination to make their marriage work. That meant they had to be honest with each other about their own part in why the previous marriage did not work. In my parents' marriage they had the usual disagreements, each of them tenaciously articulating their own side of an argument, but at the end of the day they continued to be each other's best friends. They knew how to forgive each other, even if they couldn't always say it in words. They were playful with each other. And they danced into old age with a deep love for each other. They aged well, and I find myself reliving their marriage in my own.

Couples need to pursue the success of a marriage daily and always be willing to learn from each other. Lifelong learning is essential to a good marriage. Some fifteen years ago, after twenty-five years of marriage, I finally learned what my wife meant by the word *support*, as in, "All I am asking for is your support!" This revelation came to me in the midst of a disagreement we were having over some issue long lost to my memory. A husband reading this will understand that a wife's request for support means she wants him to fix something in her life, right? Wrong! I am a good problem solver, but nothing I tried to fix *in my wife* seemed to satisfy my wife's complaint that I was not being supportive of her. In what now seems to me a humorous moment, it finally occurred to me to ask her, "What do you mean by support?" She replied, "Don't try to fix anything. Don't try to solve my problem. Just be a good listener and keep quiet as I try to work through my own problems." Since that momentous breakthrough, I have programmed myself to think, "Don't say anything, just listen," when she asks for support. There's an old proverb that applies here: "Live and learn."

A husband and wife who play together, stay together. This is especially true when they are creative about it. Life is often burdensome and, in addition to letting the Lord bear those burdens for us, we need a little comic relief. Some years ago my wife was grocery shopping and was handed a stuffed Tony the Tiger as part of a marketing give-away. The tiger had a silly expression on its face and my wife placed it in one of my dresser drawers as a surprise for me. Over the years Tony has appeared

We have been playing this game of hiding the tiger from each other for over ten years . . .

everywhere from my bookcase to under her pillow to inside our refrigerator or a coat pocket. We have been playing this game of hiding the tiger from each other for over ten years, finding enjoyment in the other's surprise discovery. As I write, Tony sits atop a gargoyle in my study where my wife placed him a week ago and where he is now waiting for me to make him appear for my wife to find elsewhere. This spontaneous play is part of our love for each other that turns up at the least expected times and places.

In addition to playfulness, friends contribute to aging well. New friends appear in our lives as new neighbors, as students at the dance studio, as people we meet in our volunteer activities. Many of our friends are much younger than we are, but that seems to keep us young as we age. We still get together with our peers, but conversations are often about our sore feet from dancing or their new knee joints because of arthritis. The delight of old friends, however, is that we we share memories as well as a future. In being surrounded by friends, and in creative play between husband and wife, and in lifelong learning together, we are also surrounded by Him who is our life, Jesus Christ, the Lord of the dance.

A Maturing Faith

At every stage in life our faith needs to grow in order for us to mature spiritually. In adolescence, a childlike faith needs to begin growing into the wisdom of a more mature faith. Jesus said we are to be like "little children" in relationship to God, but this does not mean retaining an immature faith. It means being able to love and trust in Jesus Christ in new ways throughout life. The painful, but necessary, developmental task of being a teenager is to begin to develop an identity apart from that of parents, gradually learning to think for oneself and to take responsibility for one's own life.

Spiritually, as we mature, we learn to lean more and more on God than on our parents. In early years, we wrestle spiritually with what it means to be a young man or woman of God. As a young adult we learn a more mature intimacy as we let others into our life. Eventually we share the greatest experience of human intimacy with the one who becomes our spouse. At that time there is great opportunity for spiritual growth as we share our faith with each other. So goes the way of life through events, experiences, and the grace of God that accompanies us along the way.

As we age, we have opportunity to grow in faith. Shortly after I retired, I had a dream that I was standing on a sidewalk in a suburban neighborhood similar to the one where I grew up in New Jersey. The sidewalk ended where I was standing. Beside and behind me there were homes and yards, trees and flowers, the sounds of people and traffic, but straight ahead of me there was a desert. It stretched to the horizon without plant, rock, or mountain to obstruct it. Even while dreaming, I felt that this desert was

Eventually we share the greatest experience of human intimacy with the one who becomes our spouse.

> *... do what God gives you to do now, no matter how small, and trust that He will provide for you."*

my life in retirement, and I knew the horizon was heaven awaiting me. It was not a disturbing dream, but a bewildering one. The question I heard myself say in my dream was simply, "What do I do between now and when I reach the horizon?" Some months later, in answer to that question, I wrote a note to myself, "Why do I wonder what to do with my life and become discouraged because I can't find an answer? God promises to provide something for you to do. Until that becomes clear, do what God gives you to do now, no matter how small, and trust that He will provide for you." Writing this book is part of what God apparently had in mind for me. I might also add that God's list for me seems to be unending and at times overwhelming, just as it has always been in my life. It is only by grace that we live each day continuing to learn to love and trust in God.

As we age, we increasingly experience helplessness and loss of control over our lives. This experience need not be depressing, but can turn us back to the Lord, who has promised to be our help, and who is the one in control of our lives for our good. Whether menopause and the end of childbearing, the emptiness felt when the children have grown and left home, the death of parents and the loss of friends, or even retirement and the loss of feeling needed, all transitional times in life invite us to love and trust in Jesus Christ all the more. This is not a blind trust that hides from the realities of life as we age, but an open-eyed, heads-up faith that takes on the frightening things that need to be seen for what they are if we are to entrust them to God and respond realistically.

For example, there are negatives and positives regarding retirement, just as there are at all times in life. In retirement we may have less control over our bodies and our personal world around us, but we have more time to think in faith terms. We have time to remember past joys, appreciate the present moment, and look forward to the future that is full of promise in Christ. We can still plan and accomplish, but without the pressure of the expectations of others. When we are given this opportunity by God to take charge of our lives, it is only faith fulfilling to do so. Spiritually, in retirement, this means taking charge of the opportunity to pay more attention to our personal devotional life and to prepare for public worship as the time and place where God takes charge and prepares us to serve Him in new ways. Our life with God the Father, Son, and Holy Spirit is enhanced as we depend on Him more and more in life and find even greater peace in doing so than we did before. When we are at peace, we often find that God has given us opportunity to serve Him in new ways.

As we age, we need to take advantage of the supports around us that God has provided, such as a good husband or wife, a church family, God's Word to us, and His own life that feeds us in the Sacraments. In addition to these many opportunities, God has provided pastors to care for us spiritually. Most pastors I know would prize the opportunity of providing pastoral care to their aging parishioners. At junctures of life's crises it is worth making an appointment with a pastor to speak about the fears and frustrations that face us. When I retired, my wife was not ready to have me around the house fulltime just yet. She was active in the community and at church, and the prospect of us spending twenty-four hours a day together seemed it might require limiting her commitments and activities. With my blessing, she met with our pastor and shared her dilemma. We both discovered that as much as we valued the new amount of time we had for each other, we also valued having time to ourselves.

ANTICIPATING THE DEATH OF A SPOUSE

As our dance lessons progressed, we learned more complicated patterns in which each of us danced independently for a few steps. Earlier we had learned the difference between a closed and an open position in dance. In a closed position, we are connected in frame as a couple and move together as one. In an open position, we break connection and move separately, but still in relationship to one another. The simplest form of an open position occurs when my wife does a 360-degree turn in front of me. Having made her turn, she rejoins me to reconnect in our frame together. In this particular open-position-turn we maintain hand contact with each other throughout her turn. In more complicated patterns my wife may break connection altogether and step away to do her own steps as I do mine before we reconnect in frame once again. When she does her own steps and returns to me, I must sometimes step aside and make room for her as she returns to the space where I once stood. By my making space for her and by her moving into my space, she is able to reconnect and continue the dance.

In retirement, without the pressures and responsibilities of employment, I have grown to love and appreciate my wife more than ever. My love for her continues to grow as only love can grow with the passing of time and the investment in each other's lives over forty years of marriage. A few years before I retired we spent a week at a Caribbean beach resort. Being observed by a fellow tourist, we were asked if we were newlyweds on our honeymoon. We took that as a sign that our love and delight in each other showed. As we spend more time with each other, we also begin to realize how difficult life will be when one of us dies. It is fleetingly tempting to consider distancing ourselves from each other to lessen the pain, but such anticipatory grief can prevent neither the loss nor the pain of death. Nor would we give up the delight we share now.

A husband and wife may separate from each other during the day and reconnect with each other at night. But when a spouse dies, the space left vacant by that person is a hard place for the surviving spouse to revisit. Nevertheless, something like moving into the deceased spouse's space is what needs to happen when a death occurs. In entering into that space the surviving husband or wife chooses to feel the pain of the loss, which must eventually be faced. This first painful experience of emptiness after a death is felt shortly after the funeral, when everyone has gone home, and a grieving spouse is left alone. Entering the space left by the deceased spouse is where mourning takes place. Mourning is certainly about loss, but there is more to mourning than loss.

In marriage between a Christian husband and wife the

In marriage between a Christian husband and wife the surviving spouse will be able to continue the dance of life with the Lord as stand-in partner.

surviving spouse will be able to continue the dance of life with the Lord as stand-in partner. Moving into the space left by the other means that the surviving husband or wife need not hide from the loss. He or she can face up to it and conquer it, finding the courage to do so through faith in Jesus Christ. This will not be easy. This moving into the other's space may take time and may never fully heal the loss until joined together again on that Last Day—the glorious Day of Resurrection, but with the Lord as partner the surviving spouse will learn to live with the loss. In *Aging Well*, George Vaillant writes: "Counselors sometimes forget that the . . . work of mourning is often more to remember lost loves than to say good-bye."[4] Perhaps where love has been greatest in marriage, loss is felt the greatest, but that same love may also be the greater part of the healing and recovery that occurs with time. As the familiar saying goes: It is better to have loved and lost than never to have loved at all.

As we grow older, my wife and I are increasingly aware that it is likely one of us will die before the other. Although we are both in excellent health today, a little over ten years ago my wife was diagnosed with a life threatening inoperable brain hemorrhage that was resolved only by the grace of God. The only thing for us to do was to wait and pray. We did so for four

4. Vaillant, *Aging Well*, 104.

months before the bleeding stopped and began to be absorbed. Compelled to look death in the face, we also have learned to live under the comfort of God's grace then and now. We have also

... we love because He first loved us— 1 John 4:19

learned, with some difficulty, to say to each other, "I love God more than I love you. When you leave, God's love will remain with me." These words are not easy to say, and it sounds as if we are pulling away from each other, but that is not the case. On the contrary, it allows us to love each other more, knowing that "we love because He first loved us" (1 John 4:19). His love began for each of us in our Baptism, and we have learned to love Him in return ever since.

It has been our love for God, because He first loved us, that has enabled us to love each other even during times of stress and conflict. In disagreements between us, loving God has caused us to turn to Him in repentance and to regain perspective on our marriage. When one of us enters the space vacated by the other in this life, we will not find it vacant, for the Lord will be there for us. In the resurrection, my wife and I will see each other again, not as husband and wife, but as something more. Our love for each other will be greater then than it is now, as it will be with all who are one in Christ. As much as I love my wife, I do not look to heaven to see her as my wife, but to see her with the Lord. She will see me with Him also and our joy will be greater than it is now. The focus of all of life for Christians is that "we will always be with the Lord" (1 Thessalonians 4:17).

The meaning of Christ's death on the cross is that it is

through the suffering and death of Jesus, God has overcome the separation that would have been eternal because of sinful human nature. Everything in God's Word revealed in the Scriptures ultimately points us to the cross. In the cross, we now know the heart of God toward us as sinful human beings. God has not rejected us. From the cross God tells us that even in the worst of situations He has not abandoned us. He is present with us in our grieving the death of a spouse, in our suffering as we do so, and He will be present in our own death. As mourners we move into the space left by the one who sleeps in the Lord, and we figuratively see that spouse in the arms of God. God invites us to continue the dance through life. We can take comfort in the following verses: "Precious in the sight of the LORD is the death of His saints" (Psalm 116:15); "For God alone, O my soul, wait in silence, for my hope is from Him" (Psalm 62:5); "Trust in Him at all times, O people; pour out your heart before Him; God is a refuge for us" (Psalm 62:8). He is, after all, the Lord of the Dance!

Sola Deo Gloria

we'd

WE DON'T DANCE ALONE

While my wife and I do enjoy occasionally dancing by ourselves in the living room to a favorite recording, the reality is that most of our dancing is done together with other couples on a dance or ballroom floor. It is my role to lead my wife around the floor without crashing into the other dancers. In a very real way they become part of our dance as we include them in our movements. In the dance that is marriage, many couples will find that they, too, don't dance alone. With the blessing of children, a couple finds that it is important to add the skills of parenting to their dance as man and wife.

Dancing is contagious and was passed on to me by my parents.

The desire to dance was passed on to me by my parents. The bug lay dormant within me for almost sixty-five years before manifesting the first serious symptoms. However, once exposed to dance instruction, there was a full-blown outbreak infecting both my wife and me that now threatens to spread to our family and friends. For my wife and me, the contagion has had a curious side effect in that it has reversed parent-child roles. Our dance instructors are young enough to be our children, but they have become our parents in dance.

Recently, we performed a waltz at our dance studio before an audience of about sixty people. As we came off the floor to very generous applause, our youngest instructor (in her twenties) greeted us with the exuberant expression: "My babies!" It was easy for me to appreciate her delight in us as her students because I have long since thought of the young adults I teach each semester as "my kids." I am convinced that, whether in dance or in the classroom, it would be difficult not to care deeply for those we teach. In marriage, we become teachers to those we care about most deeply, our children. The major portion of this chapter on *parenting* is about being teacher-parents to our children, but at each end of the chapter I would like to place a bookend. The first bookend is about re-parenting yourself and the second is about *parenting your parents*. In these bookends I suggest some thoughts about a version of parenting to which we may not have devoted much thought. I hope it is helpful.

Re-parenting Yourself

Dancing is contagious and was passed on to me by my parents.

Parenting is contagious! Unless we make a conscious decision otherwise, we will parent our children the way we were parented. It may have been good parenting or not so good parenting. For most, it has been a little of both. Although we can read and study how to be good parents, it is actually in parenting our own children that we learn the most. If we have been parented well, much of what we received will become good for our children. But there are always those things in each of us that we would like to do differently than our parents. Therefore, as we parent our children, we also need to learn to re-parent ourselves. Re-parenting ourselves means first learning to evaluate and choose how we want to respond to the way we were parented. If not, we will automatically do what our parents did.

For example, I was a very small child, smaller than all my friends and classmates until ninth grade. As happens among boys, bigger boys sometimes bullied me. On many occasions I complained to my mother that I was too small to fight off the bullies. My mother's response was, "If you can't reach his nose, hit him in the belly!" With the ambivalence of shame and pride I have to admit that I once carried out my mother's advice and became an instant hero among my smaller peers. But the message in my mother's words was both good and bad. The good message: "Don't be afraid to stand up to bullies." The bad message: "Use violence to do so." I don't recall whether I recommended my mother's advice to my own children, but if I did not it was only because the love of God controlled me (see 2 Corinthians 5:14). My mother was empathetic and supportive toward me, even if her advice in this case was questionable.

My example fails to illustrate the most damaging message parents pass on when they communicate to their children that they are unwanted, unloved, or get in the way of a parent's life. This is a harmful and difficult message to erase and replace with something better. Re-parenting has to take place to avoid being the same way to our own children some-day. To evaluate the messages we pass on, we must observe how we speak and act toward our children. Being an observer of oneself requires that we actively think about what we are doing. As simple as this sounds, it is not easy to be objective at the moment of crisis. Even if we evaluate our behavior after-ward, it is hard to be fair and not be defensive with ourselves and our children.

To get more help in evaluating our parenting we might ask someone we respect to observe us over a period of time. This may be a neighbor or friend, but not our own parent(s). This willingness to open up our lives and to see ourselves as others see us is part of growing toward greater maturity. The feedback we get from others will naturally be disruptive to our usual way of handling things. We will have to put aside our instant response of rejecting painful insights. We will need to give ourselves time to ask and answer, "Is that really what I am doing to my kids?" The next question we will need to ask is, "*Why* do I do that?" The answer may be, "That's the way my parents did it," or "It's my overreaction to what my parents did." The final question we need to ask is, "What do I want to do differently?" Even with seriously considering these questions and answers, we still need support from others to make the change. Husbands and wives need to support each other in their growing maturity as parents.

There are always some obstacles to re-parenting ourselves. When our dance instructors teach us something difficult, I tend to become impatient with myself. However, my teachers do not become impatient. They realize that new things are difficult to learn. But I learned impatience from my father. While growing up I resented my father's impatience and his way of showing it, only to find myself being the same way with my children. It was only as I became a parent and realized how much I disliked myself for being that way that I decided to work at re-parenting myself. The first thing I had to do was to forgive my father for his impatience. As I learned to do this, I was also able to confess and find forgiveness for my own impatience. In time, my impatience, which also showed itself outside the home, began to change into something else. Feedback from others said that I showed *alacrity* in my work. Alacrity means *cheerful eagerness*. Alacrity is the other side of the coin of *impatience*. I still have to confront my impatience at times, but apparently alacrity has become my more dominant side of the coin.

As we grow in love and forgiveness toward our parents for what they have been to us in their weakness, then we will be prepared to parent our children out of our strength rather than our weakness. Reconciliation with parents begins with our own reconciliation with God, for when we have been forgiven, we will also grow in forgiving others. The Gospel of our reconciliation with God transforms us from within, enabling God's grace to make the changes in us that we cannot make alone.

Parenting Your Children

Parenting is a process of having authority over our children to enjoying friendship with them. From infancy through adolescence they need our authority, but from young adulthood on they increasingly need our friendship. As parents, we need to teach our children how to develop this relationship. The commandment given by God to "[h]onor your father and your mother" (Exodus 20:12) affirms our authority as teacher-parents. A child's obedience to his parent's teaching authority is obedience to the authority of God: "Children, obey your parents in the Lord, for this is right" (Ephesians 6:1). The line of authority in the home runs from God to the husband; from the husband to the wife; and from both husband and wife as parents to their children. As in the relationship of a husband toward his wife, this authority is not to be authoritarian in nature, but is to be exercised with patience and love. This authority is tempered in marriage and in parenting by God's warning: "Husbands, love your wives, and do not be harsh with them," and "Fathers, do not provoke your children, lest they become discouraged" (Colossians 3:19, 21). Parents need to learn to exercise their authority in firmness with love, and children need to learn to obey their parents, who act in God's behalf, without resentment.

The fact that parents could at any moment exercise firmness that lacks love or that children could show obedience without honor for their parents only attests to the need for God's forgiveness and the need for our forgiveness toward one another. Parents need to model forgiveness in words and actions that help their children honor them as parents. In doing so, parents model God's discipline and teach their children to honor God. As such, the aim of parenting is to "bring [children] up in the discipline and instruction of the Lord" (Ephesians 6:4). We must teach our children to live the right way rather than the wrong way. Children who are taught to live in God's love and under His grace have a better chance of becoming spiritually mature as they grow up.

As children grow older they need to be given as much authority as they can responsibly handle. My grandson showed interest in my daughter's cooking and asked if he could help. He eventually learned how to make scrambled eggs, French toast, and refrigerated cinnamon rolls, and now, at the age of six, he makes breakfast for the family on Sunday mornings. Not all children will be able to do this, but where children show aptitude and interest in doing something they can responsibly handle, parents ought to encourage it.

This handing over of responsibility at the level of a child's demonstrated competence builds self-confidence in the child. My father had good intentions when he invited me to watch him use his power tools. Unfortunately, he did not allow me hands-on experience with power tools and it was not until adulthood that I gained the confidence to attempt minor repairs around the house. Parents may have good intentions, but may not realize how children actually learn. Because my father was deeply devoted to me and meant well, I respected him even in his failed attempts to teach me. In coming to this realization, I have become kinder to myself when recalling my own failed attempts in teaching my children.

Parents must also give responsibility, and therefore authority, to children to practice their faith in the home. It is ultimately a father's responsibility, supported by his wife, to teach children how to do this. Our children grew up with a table prayer before meals and an after-dinner evening devotion around the table. There were a few nights when this did not happen due to neglect or some pressing need, but there were more nights than not when it did happen. We took time to share the faith and talk about the day's experiences. This was never coerced or forced on our children, though there were times when each of us struggled against human nature to remain at the table. These times for reading the Bible and other devotional helps frequently turned into lengthy discussions in answer to questions our children raised. There were times when we were asked difficult questions and had to speak those humbling words a parent fears most, "I don't know." Honest faith shared with children is better than mere knowledge with little or no faith. As children mature they learn that faith is not a matter of having all the answers to life's questions, but a matter of learning to love and trust in Christ above all things.

We tried to make our table time together a time for our children to come to us with things on their minds they had learned from friends or at school. We tried to listen without reacting defensively as authoritarian guardians of the faith.

Although we set limits under God's Law, our aim was to help them see the Gospel of Christ as that which transforms us to live this life with hope and joy. For our failings as teachers we tried to teach our children to forgive and for our successes we tried to teach them to be thankful for the grace of God at work in us all.

Parenting our children means preparing them to think for themselves in their relationship with God in Jesus Christ. This does not mean encouraging them to invent their own spirituality or their own ideas of how they would like to think of God. Rather, it means coming face-to-face with God in Jesus Christ in their lives. But there is a difficulty in parents trying to pass on the faith. There is an objective side to faith comprised of what Christians have always believed according to the Word of God, the Bible. And there is a subjective side of faith expressed as that which I like best about the faith. The goal of passing on the faith is to pass on the objective Truth about Jesus Christ, while allowing the subjective response to evolve within each of us. Of course, when the subjective takes precedent over the objective, then our subjective must surrender to the objective Truth and not to our own likes and dislikes. For example, when a child complains about being bored during worship services, a parental response is not to keep the child at home, but to help the child find something in the service to look for. Parents might read and discuss a portion of the Bible reading before the service, suggesting that they listen for it. A parent might teach a child a hymn that will be sung. The Apostles' Creed could be taught at home so that the child can participate in confessing it with the congregation. Lessons and hymns for the next Sunday can be obtained from the church office during the week. Expression of faith must always serve the authority of the objectivity of the Word of God in worship and in life.

Each of us finds something in the Christian faith that becomes attached to our way of expressing it. This way of holding on to our faith is called our personal *piety*. Piety is the personal expression of how we devote ourselves to God. Piety is personal, but must always be subject to the objectivity of Christ and the Word of God.[1] When I was a teenager, I liked spirituals in the style of country music, but I also liked the chorales I heard in church services as a style of classical music. I enjoyed spirituals as part of my personal piety at home and chorales as more appropriate for worship services. Spirituals expressed my subjective feelings, but the chorales in worship services gave objectivity to my faith with meaning deeper than I could know alone.

The difficulty in passing on the faith to our children is that we pass on both our piety and our objective faith, sometimes making them indistinguishable. Piety may be genuine, but it is faulty because it is flavored with our own personality as a parent that may not be the same as that of our children. For example, a parent whose piety is connected to excessiveness in commitment to congregational activities, to the exclusion of time for his children, may convey the message that being faithful to God means sacrificing time with your children. Consequently, children may understandably grow up to resent

....
1. Piety should be distinguished from Pietism, which is associated with a rigidity that demands everyone's piety be the same.

their parent's commitments to the faith. It may be that a parent's excessive involvement in congregational activities has more to do with the need to escape obligations at home, the need for success and approval from others, or the need to exercise control over things, than it does with their zeal for the Lord. Each person's faith is expressed, in part, according to his or her needs, and children find difficulty in separating the personal and personality of their parents from the objective faith in Christ. The task of a child in becoming a mature adult is to learn to make the distinction between the substance of faith and the parental form in which they experienced it as a child. Passing on the faith to our children will inevitably include our piety, but more importantly it must also include the objectivity of the Gospel and Christ's love for them.

TIME WITH OUR CHILDREN

Parents need time with their children especially from infancy through teen years. As difficult as it may be for families to find time to eat dinner together, there needs to be an agreement within the family that this is a necessary and worthwhile thing to do. Dinnertime is a social event, a time to be relaxed with each other. It is intellectually, spiritually, and physically healthy to eat together. As children grow up, parents need to protect a child's time at home from the deluge of activities pulling them away from family. This includes not letting ourselves or our children become so involved in activities that there is little time left for each other at home. Parents need to set limits for their children, helping them to learn to say "no" to endless urgings outside the home.

At the beginning of each school year my wife and I would assist our children in choosing two or three activities at school or in the community in which to be active in addition to Sunday School and worship services at church. This allowed us to schedule family time. Our own children later voluntarily turned down Sunday morning job offers and activities that interfered with their participation in the life of the Church at worship. Just as we need dinnertime together at home, so also we need to gather with the Body of Christ, the Church, to be fed by God each week. Whether toddlers or teens, the time to set the pattern is now. It is easier to make exceptions to this rule, but virtually impossible to agree to time together when exceptions have been the rule all along. As children become teenagers they need to be participants in working out time spent with the family. Time together at the dinner table (or whenever else) needs to be a positive experience, which means that the children ought to be permitted to participate in taking the lead in prayer, readings, and discussions, voicing their opinions and ultimately raising questions of faith and life.

FRIENDSHIP WITH OUR CHILDREN

Early in our marriage my wife and I joined a parent's growth group. The leader of the group, a Methodist minister and psychologist, suggested that we should aim at making our adult children our best friends by the way we raise them. He cited his relationship with his young adult son and their mutual eagerness to hike and travel together by canoe in the wilderness. He was quick to clarify that this did not mean that parents ought to relate to their young children as friends. Friendships occur between peers; young children are not peers to their parents. But friendship between parents and their adult children can develop later if children have been prepared for it while growing up. Parents, for example, ought to have good times with their children, times for honest discussion as well as play. This prepares them for being friends later on. The opposite is also true. Parents should not alienate their children by dominating, ridiculing, or undermining self-confidence, something easy to do because children are vulnerable and nearly always at our mercy.

The final stage in making our emerging adult children our friends is to let go of them as they become older adolescents and young adults. It is the responsibility of both parents and their adult children to make this happen gradually. Parents need to stop telling their sons and daughters how to live their lives and sons and daughters need to stop depending on their parents for their lingering childhood needs. It is hard for parents, when they have enjoyed their children's companionship, to let go of their children in this final way so that they come back to them as peers and therefore friends. This "letting go" is a mindset on the part of the parent who willingly withholds words of advice to adult children unless they ask for it. As parents do this, they allow sons and daughters to claim authority for their lives as adults. When this happens, adult children are learning to become adult friends with their parents. Sensing something has changed in the nature of their relationship with their parents, adult children will sometimes test their parents to see if this something is genuine. Testing may cause tension between them as they try to live differently with each other.

Until the testing is over and both sides can accept this new relationship, both parents and children stand painfully poised on the threshold that separates a parent-child relationship from a peer-friend relationship.

PARENTING YOUR CHILDREN

Parenting children is not the most daunting experience in life; parenting our parents is more so. As parents we may find ourselves in an interesting predicament as we age. Not only will we have been a parent to our children, but we may also become the parent of our own aging parents. Although "obeying mother and father" ends with the onset of adulthood, "honoring mother and father" continues throughout a lifetime. Honoring parents sometimes means parenting our parents when they can no longer manage their own lives adequately.

An advertisement from an assisted living facility addressed to middle aged adult children asks the question, "Have you noticed anything different about your parents?"

As we came off the floor to very generous applause, our youngest instructor (in her twenties) greeted us with the exuberant expression: "My babies!"

The brochure encourages us to ask ourselves questions about how our aging parents are managing their checkbook, trash disposal, meal preparation, personal grooming, medications, and other daily tasks. These things may be indicators of an aging parent's inability to manage their needs without help. The implication is that it may be time for us as an adult son or daughter to take charge of our parent's welfare and provide assistance. It is not easy for our parents, or for us as their sons and daughters, to admit this need for a reversal of roles. When signs of dementia are evident in an aging parent and there is no one else in the home capable of caring for that person, the need for a reversal of roles in parenting clearly demands our attention. When aging parents are mentally healthy but physical limitations increase, it may be hard for parents to admit their need for assistance. Even when they are open to it, the course of action may not be easy to negotiate.

Signs that our parents need our help usually become clear first to our spouse. Harry had always been attached to his mother, and as she aged he became more attached, fearing for her well-being. Although he spent more time with his mother and less time with his wife, he denied the need to consider a nursing home. It was only when his wife confronted him with his neglect of her needs as his wife that he realized his unwillingness to take charge of his mother's welfare by placing her where she could be safe and comfortable. We have grown up seeing our parents as parents and it may not even occur to us that the time for a reversal of roles is at hand. The first intervention usually takes the form of trying to be reasonable with the parent and offering to do things for them. Normally, this would be appropriate, but as more and more intervention is needed and our time is increasingly taken up with a parent's needs, it becomes clear that our roles must change.

It may be that wives, as mothers and caregivers for their children, may be more willing to take on the care of their parents. In so doing, a wife must be careful not to neglect the time she and her husband need in order to maintain their own marriage. Parents living in the home of their adult sons or daughters do have an influence on them that is not always easily identifiable and that may be detrimental at times. Husbands must be careful not to become more devoted to their mothers than to their wives, always remembering, "a man shall leave his father and his mother and hold fast to his wife" (Genesis 2:24). *Leaving* does not mean abandoning parents; it means *honoring* them by doing what is best for them and also for their own marriage. Both husbands and wives must learn that their devotion to each other takes first place, and honoring their parents slightly less than *first place*, even if a bit more than second place.

In dancing, if a couple maintains their frame, the steps they take and the patterns they follow will work well for them. If a couple has worked at developing a wholesome, loving marriage with awareness of each other's needs, they will then be better prepared to face the problem of parenting aging parents. In my own case, as the years went by, my mother had an increasingly difficult time adjusting to the death of my father. As my wife took on more and more of the care for my mother because I was occupied with obligations at work, I began to realize the affect this was having on my wife's health. Consequently, I suggested we look for an assisted living facility and arrange for ways to involve my mother in our family life within the framework of meeting our own needs as well. This was not easy, but it was the right thing to do for my mother and my wife. We honor our parents when we provide for their welfare even when they complain about it, as we did when we were children and they were parenting us.

SOME CLOSING THOUGHTS

We parent one another because God first parented us. It is part of our being *like God* that we parent our children and perhaps our own parents someday. Not all marriages produce children, but all marriages have had parents who brought us into this world. Parenting is a way of teaching us to care for one another. Caring is not always easy, as any young mother will tell us. Nor is caring for aging parents easy when the burden we have been to them in our youth now shifts to our shoulders in caring for them in their old age. In either case, it is our vocation to "bear one another's burdens" (Galatians 6:2). God always cares for us. His love is unending. His mercy is new every morning. His generosity is eternal. We are his likeness to one another as we re-parent ourselves, our children, and our parents.

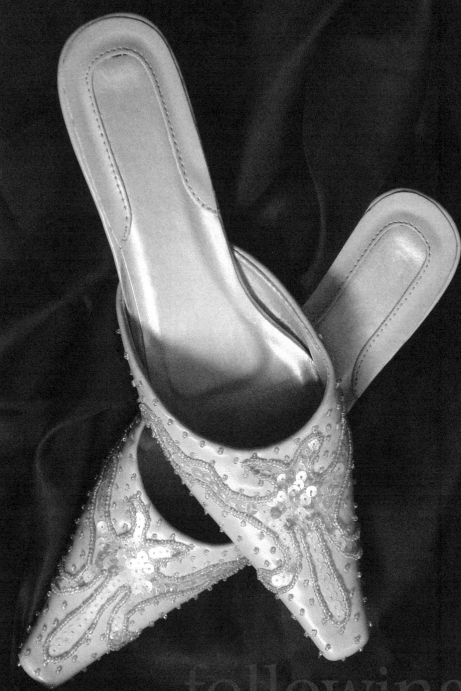

following

FOLLOWING HIS LEAD

AFTERWORD BY SUSAN EYER

I was born into the poverty of having non-dancing parents. I didn't know what I was missing but, like most kids, I loved dancing around the living room to music that came from the radio or records. Fortunately, my parents did provide us kids with a rich exposure to classical music. For me the thought of actually taking dance lessons with my husband seemed impossible at first. I always thought of myself as a klutz; in college I was assigned to take remedial ball throwing as part of a physical education course. However, confronted by our

Marriage is truly a balancing act for the wife . . .

enthusiastic, as well as patient, dance teachers and my husband's delight as we maneuvered through the first few weeks of lessons, I began to catch the fun in this new challenge in order to shed self-consciousness and develop confidence in my physical ability to do anything resembling a sport.

Given my background, I found it comforting to learn that the man's responsibility in ballroom dance is to lead and the woman's is to follow. While I've supported and tried to live out the same principle in marriage, I can say that following is very hard work indeed. Marriage is truly a balancing act for the wife between being majorly responsible as leader for the children in the home and/or for others in the workplace, and being equally responsible for following the lead of her husband for the good of the marriage. Sometimes we women manage that well and sometimes badly. It is not always easy for me to keep my balance in the dance of life.

Even our dance instructors tell their students that the biggest challenge for women is to learn to follow the man's lead. I will attempt to address this particular issue from my vantage point. For any woman who is bright, educated, and gifted, it is not easy to submit to the idea of having to follow her husband's lead. Yet the metaphor of ballroom dancing has helped me understand and appreciate more than ever what it means for me to follow my husband's lead. I often have to learn more steps than he in a complicated choreography because the woman does the fancy, showy stuff of turns and spins. I cannot just go off on my own and do them whenever

I feel like it. I must be led into a turn or spin. In fact, I can only turn or spin when my husband leads me by throwing me off-balance ever so slightly. My responsibility is to respond immediately to keep in time to the music and to "collect myself," regaining my balance in order to continue the dance.

In marriage a wife needs to be so in tune with her husband that she picks up on his throwing her off-balance, so to speak. This is a wild concept. Being thrown off-balance is not comfortable! It can happen in any number of ways. When a husband becomes so absorbed or burdened down with his work outside the home, a wife is thrown off-balance. When he fails to see and provide for her needs for support, intimacy, and help with the children, she again is thrown off-balance. She often finds herself in a spin she didn't see coming. She can complain and resent her husband, or she can see the opportunity to bring good out of the situation. One way she can respond is by "collecting herself" and gently reminding her husband of his leadership in the family. In loving communication he and she can work out details for her to hold down the fort or take on some of his usual home duties temporarily for a specific, delegated, agreed upon time period.

About twenty-four years into our marriage, my husband asked me to fill in at his chaplain's office while his secretary took a seven-week maternity leave. He led me into this complicated turn by talking about the challenge several months ahead of time. He supported me through these weeks that also included our children's graduations, one from college and one from high school, and all the attendant festivities. We were still adjusting as a family to the planned move of our in-laws into

. . . the best marriages flourish when the husband leads and the wife follows

our home the previous month. On top of all that I was the chief trainer for our puppy in a twelve-week obedience school during wet, spring weather. At the time the whole family pitched in by helping with meals, taking Grandma and Grandpa to the doctor, and training the dog. It was only when we looked back that we could see that hectic but memorable time as my shining hour: a series of spins and spiral turns. Likewise, God Himself sometimes leads both husbands and wives into spins we didn't see coming. At times He throws us off-balance in order to challenge us to trust His leading above anything else. After all, He can see ahead where we cannot. This is the hard work of following our Lord in faith and faithfulness. He promises a good outcome to all who love Him in Christ Jesus.

In conversation with women from 30 to 90 years of age, I've discovered that many wives are slow to realize the burden of responsibility their husbands carry for the whole household. We are often so aware of all the many aspects of family life that we as women hold ourselves accountable for that we fail to appreciate how much our husbands plan for the future, how much they figure out how to make ends meet, and how much they care to protect their families from any threat or danger. Men want and need their wives' respect and trust in order to lead their wives and children effectively—to provide and to protect them physically, financially, emotionally, and spiritually.

In most marriages today it appears that men and women share leadership mutually. In reality, the best marriages flourish when the husband leads and the wife follows. Both indeed function best as one when each is strong at the core and maintains an internal balance. The way a wife follows is by learning and practicing her part well and encouraging her husband's leadership. The best way of encouraging him, strengthening his role as husband and father, is to pray for him daily. Another way is what I call "percolating time." I have learned through trial and error that when I have a new, good idea that I think would benefit our marriage or family, I must be willing to plant the seed of the idea in a non-threatening, non-accusatory way, and give it time to percolate in my husband's mind. That way it allows him to take the lead in considering the option I've suggested and deciding whether to implement it or not after including me in the reasons and resolution. I used to think that some of my ideas weren't worth much because I expected immediate recognition of my wisdom or insight. Yes, it's hard to wait for direction. I've learned to trust my husband to see the bigger picture. He often looks to me for the details. The result is a better partnership.

To continue the theme of the man leading and the woman following, I will cite an example our dance instructor demonstrated to show how to follow. He asked me to be ready to snap my fingers at exactly the same time he snapped his. I tried and tried but just couldn't do it. I always had to start just a split second after I saw and heard his snap. To anyone else it may have looked and sounded like we were snapping our fingers at the same time, just as it may look like two are dancing as one. In fact the man leads and the woman follows only a split second behind him.

In order to be so connected with each other, both the man and the woman in ballroom dancing must "keep the frame" in order for the woman to see and feel the man's lead. Both have to be strong partners at the core without overpowering the other. Even when both partners are "in frame" and have the proper hand connections and body alignment, there is a big temptation for the woman who knows her part as well as the man's part to "back-lead". Back-leading happens when a woman who usually travels backward acts aggressively by pulling the man according to her stride and thus interrupting his leadership. This is dangerous because she cannot see where she is going. The man must lead and even gauge the size of their steps in order to avoid mishaps on the dance floor.

In marriage it is dangerous for the wife to back-lead. If she alone tries to determine the direction and agenda for the marriage, she ends up pulling her husband to match her stride and so sabotages his leadership. In gently calling each other to account, one allows the other to reflect, apologize, and start over. In theological terms this translates to mutual repentance, confession, and absolution in the setting of the home. Trust and respect are restored. When things go well, and a marriage is fed and nurtured by forgiveness and special, good times together, we can call this a Virtuous Cycle. When complaining to and about each other, criticizing each other, and avoiding each other are the order of the day, we can call these a Vicious Cycle. All marriages experience both. By the grace of God the virtuous memories help sustain us through the vicious, spiraling-down times we all have come to know.

Husbands and wives need to get away together alone

occasionally in order to build up a reservoir of good times and memories. This reality seems almost unthinkable when the kids are young. It is well worth the effort in the long run to find sitters, plan menus, and prime the youngsters for the parents' absence. We used to tell our children when they were in middle school years and older that we needed to go out to dinner alone so that we could be a better mom and a better dad to them when we came back home. They got to the point of sending us off with a cheerful, "Have a good time." Sometimes on a rare getaway weekend, after planned or serendipitous fun, we would set aside time to talk about ourselves: our projects and problems, our dreams and goals and hobbies, what we saw in ourselves that we wanted to change for the better, and our busy schedules and the need to spend time with extended family. We made notes of the changes we wanted to make so that we could return home and focus on solutions. For example, I remember at one of our getaways, my husband said he was tired of seeing me wear the same dark green jacket whenever we went out. He encouraged me to buy some new clothes! I tended to be too frugal in shopping for clothes for myself. He had figured there was enough money in the budget for that, so I only had to follow his lead and jazz up the dance.

You can imagine my surprise and delight when, about six months into dance lessons, I realized that I really enjoyed dancing and could actually perform some graceful moves. And my legs didn't feel like shaky, bamboo rods trying to move to music. About sixteen years into marriage I fully appreciated the fact that I really was the best wife my husband could have. That realization came about after many conversations with women friends who were going through a lot of turmoil in their marriages, leading either to divorce or to counseling and renewal. My part in our marriage certainly was not always graceful but was always sustained by the grace of God to counsel me through His Word, renew me in forgiveness, and lead me in closer communication with my husband.

The most graceful dancer I knew most of my life was my mother-in-law. She had danced since she was a young girl. Her movements on the dance floor were elegant. If I ever compared myself to her, I knew I could never dance the way she did. In fact I didn't even consider dancing a thing I could ever do. I must have assumed that she was born knowing how to dance and I wasn't. I do know now that it takes hard work for anyone to dance well; I just have to practice more and work even harder to translate what I know and understand in my brain to my leg, arm, and core body muscles. There is something called "muscle memory" that dancers, athletes, and pianists know. When one has learned a pattern, a move, or a recital piece well—up to performance caliber, that person can recall that pattern or piece without too much effort months or years later because the leg, arm, or finger muscles have retained a memory of the particulars through repeated, correct practice.

A well-seasoned marriage compares favorably to the muscle memory analogy. In practicing the many moves of marriage in the lead/follow tandem, muscle memory takes over when we meet the same problems or challenges again or in a slightly different presentation. What we learned the hard way when we were newly married often becomes easier as we mature. In other words, if and as we age well, we find more comfort and more enjoyment in each other. My dear husband still leads and I still follow in the dance of marriage. Both leading and following require hard work and humility before each other and before God.

DISCUSSION GUIDES FOR HUSBAND AND WIFE[1]

CHAPTER ONE

Marriage is not whatever we choose to make of it, but is what God has made it to be! The following discussion questions are offered to help clarify this:

1. After reading this chapter, how would each of you describe what marriage is in your own words?
2. Is your attitude toward marriage influenced by what you see and hear about marriage on television or among your friends?
3. How is a husband "like God" and a wife "like God" in marriage according to this chapter?
4. Marriage is a one flesh union between husband and wife. What does this mean and NOT mean according to this chapter?
5. How is marriage like the relationship between Christ and the Church according to this chapter?

Concluding thought: This chapter raises many questions about the uniqueness of marriage as a one-of-a-kind relationship. Be sure you have understood this chapter as a way to understand the more personal part of marriage covered in the next chapter guides.

CHAPTER TWO

In marriage, as in ballroom dancing, the husband must lead and the wife must follow. Regardless of the cultural changes in the acceptance or rejection of this ordering of marriage, it is the way God has made marriage to be.

1. In your marriage who leads and who follows most of the time?

---

1. This is not a guide for discussion in groups, but only for husband and wife personally.

2. What problems do you see in taking the lead as a husband?
3. What problems do you see in following your husband's lead?
4. In what circumstances do you as husband fail to lead where you should?
5. What would help each of you to overcome problems in leading or following?
6. In what ways might you as a husband delegate leadership to your wife without abandoning your responsibility to ultimately take the lead in marriage?

Chapter Three

"The man is always in the wrong" is a saying in dancing that means that when his partner doesn't follow his lead and goes her own way, it is usually because he isn't leading her well. It is assumed in dancing that the man is responsible for both of them.

1. What do you think of this saying as applied to your marriage?
2. How did each (set) of your parents settle disagreements in their marriage?
3. What does each of you contribute to a bad argument? How can you correct it?
4. What do you want from each other when you disagree?
5. What do you think of the statement, "When one of you has a problem, both of you have a problem." (refer to the chapter if necessary)
6. What rules can you agree to for working out conflicts in your marriage in the future?
7. Can you admit when you are wrong and say, "I'm sorry?"

Can you also say, "I forgive you" to each other?

Chapter Four

Sexual desire as sensuality is part of God's design for human beings, but God intends that a man and woman wait until marriage to fully explore their own sensuality and have sexual intercourse.

1. If you did not wait until marriage to fully explore your sensuality, tell each other how you feel about that now.
2. How has your sensual desire for each other changed over the years? Has it matured? How?
3. Is there anything you would like to see different about making love together?
4. Tell each other what you find wholesomely sensual about each other.
5. After being married for a while, what do you now find most sensually attractive about your husband/wife?
6. What do you appreciate most about each other in your marriage that has helped your relationship as husband and wife?

Chapter Five

In order to make marriage a gracious dance through life, husband and wife must worship God together and recognize that they are part of the *Body of Christ and individually members of it.*

1. If you attend public worship together, tell each other what it means to you to have him/her there with you. If you

don't attend, and your partner does, ask your attending partner how she/he feels about that.

2. If you have personal devotions alone at home, talk about what this means to you to your spouse. If one of you doesn't, have him/her talk about why.

3. If you pray at home personally together, talk about what this means to you for your marriage. If you don't pray together, talk about why you don't.

4. What do your spiritual connections of public worship and personal prayer at home do for your marriage?

5. Close this discussion with prayer, each contributing something in the prayer about the other.

CHAPTER SIX

Marriage fulfills the need for intimate companionship and promotes confidence because we feel secure in our marriage, so a husband and wife will be able to reach out beyond themselves to others.

1. What is it about your marriage that *enables* you to reach out to serve others in the neighborhood, the community, or the world?

2. We have to move about in the world, not always in each other's presence, but always on each other's mind. What does this mean to each of you?

3. How is your marriage a witness to Christ when you are out socially with others?

4. Infidelity is not so much the *cause* of marriage problems as it is the *result* of something gone wrong in the marriage.

Is there anything going wrong in your marriage that might lead to infidelity?

5. Do you, as a man with other men, talk about your spouse? Do you as a woman with other women talk about your spouse? In what way? Do you say anything that the other would find objectionable?

6. If answering any of the above questions has caused injury, pray for forgiveness together from God and from each other.

CHAPTER SEVEN

This chapter talks about aging, maturing in faith, and the death of a spouse. Although none of us finds these topics easy to discuss, what we have to say to each other is usually very important and can draw a husband and wife together.

1. In the study identified in this chapter, a good marriage at age 50 predicted positive aging at age 80. What do you think are the positive signs of aging?

2. What have you learned about yourself from you husband/wife since you have been married?

3. What do you do to have fun together (other than sex)?

4. Is aging a positive or a negative for you? Talk about why.

5. In what ways do you think your faith has matured as you have aged?

6. Have you ever talked about the death of the other to each other? Try it now, as hard as it may be to do so. Include talk about your faith in Christ.

Chapter Eight

1. Re-parenting yourself means, first, learning to evaluate and choose how you want to respond to the way you were raised. What things did each of your parents do well in parenting you? What did they not do well?

2. What do you wish you had done (or are now doing) differently in parenting your children?

3. Do you spend as much time with your children as they need from each of you? Do you *listen* to them when they speak to you?

4. Are you friends with your adult children or just parents? Why or why not?

5. Honoring parents sometimes means parenting your parents when they can no longer manage their own lives adequately. Do you see a need to parent your parents? If so, what are the reasons?

6. If you are parenting your parents, what is the hardest thing about it for each of you?